THE OVAL WINDOW

J.H. PRYNNE

THE OVAL WINDOW

A NEW ANNOTATED EDITION
BY **N.H. REEVE & RICHARD KERRIDGE**

BLOODAXE BOOKS

ISBN: 978 1 78037 126 9

First published 2018 by
Bloodaxe Books Ltd,
Eastburn,
South Park,
Hexham,
Northumberland NE46 1BS.

www.bloodaxebooks.com
For further information about Bloodaxe titles
please visit our website or write to
the above address for a catalogue.

Supported using public funding by
ARTS COUNCIL
ENGLAND

Cover design: Neil Astley & Pamela Robertson-Pearce.

Digital reprint of the 2018 Bloodaxe Books edition.

CONTENTS

Acknowledgements

J.H. Prynne kindly supplied the photographs reproduced in this volume, and a portfolio of references and source materials to help facilitate the annotation. Natalie Reeve assisted with the proofs and page references. J.H. Prynne and Tracy Kerridge read parts of the book and gave valuable advice. It would not have been possible to complete this work without the unfailing support of Cheryl Reeve.

The text of *The Oval Window* is reprinted from J.H. Prynne's *Poems*, third edition (Bloodaxe Books, 2015).

Author's dedication: I dedicate this book to the team who have worked on it with such persistent and exacting scruple: editors Neil Reeve and Richard Kerridge, and publisher Neil Astley. Their labour gives a new sense to the word dedication and I record my gratitude for this commitment to the continuing life of poetry.

Reading *The Oval Window*

If we are looking for conventional linear sense, the opening lines are disconcerting. They present us with discontinuities and obscure technical terms:

> The shut inch lively as pin grafting
> leads back to the gift shop, at a loss
> for two-ply particles
>   set callow,
> set bland and clean, wailing as when
> to wait is block for scatter. Ah so,
> the estrangement of the cause brings off
> a surcease of the affect, even end-up
> battered in sawdust. You cut your chin
> on all this, like club members on the dot
> by a winter blaze.
>   What can't be helped
> is the vantage, private and inert; yet
> in a twinkling mind you, to pick up
> elastic replacements on the bench code.

Since the publication of this long poem in 1983, a transformative development for the practice of reading has occurred: the availability of the internet and of search engines such as Google. This change is especially important for readers of texts of this kind – texts that include a wider variety of specialist language than any reader is likely to understand without research. Such language is highly technical, and, much of the time, readers may compromise by contenting themselves with recognising the general source of the terminology rather than proceeding to investigate the specific meaning of each piece. Phrases from financial columns in newspapers, computer programming or surgery are recognised firstly as samples, whose initial meaning consists of the general moral, political and cultural aura of these systems and practices, as perceived by the reader, who may then investigate the particular words if the time is available.

Commentators have sometimes positioned Prynne and Philip Larkin as opposites. Several did so in the flurry of debate in national newspapers and on BBC Radio 4's *Today* programme stirred up by the publication in 2004 of Randall Stevenson's *The Last of England?*, a critical survey of literature published in Britain between 1960 and 2000. To the indignation of some critics, Stevenson had given roughly equal space to Prynne and Larkin, treating Prynne too as one of the finest and most important poets of the period. In such arguments, Larkin is used as the representative of the values of the Movement writers of the 1950s and 60s, especially their hostility to Modernist innovations in literary form and to writing that confronted readers with immediate linguistic difficulty. Movement writers favoured what they characterised as recognisable ordinary language, combined in poetry with traditional metrical and stanzaic form. They hoped that works written in this way might recover for poetry some of the popular readership and cultural centrality that had been lost since the previous century. Prynne's decision to turn in a contrasting direction, towards Modernist 'open' forms not restricted by the need for a stable dramatic voice, can be seen as a response to a quite different perception of poetry's marginalisation. He began to take this new direction in the middle to late 1960s, after relinquishing a style that was closer to Movement writing.

The poem written in plain, easily recognised, broadly shared language, as advocated by Movement writers, would nearly always take the dramatic form of a monologue or soliloquy. There would be a single speaker or persona, a 'point of view' in the terminology of the Creative Writing classroom, drama-tised as uttering reflections arising from an experience or set of experiences described in the poem, or from long consideration of a topic. The turn, or movement of thought and feeling, seems to take place as we read, as if the poem really were a spontaneous piece of life. This movement carries the work to a point of dramatic conclusion at which the poet naturally breaks off, though of course we do not necessarily experience a gentle touchdown or persuasive intellectual resolution. At each subsequent reading, the sense of spontaneity is there again: the event will be different, because the moment in the reader's life is different, but the shifts of feeling will still seem to be real events in a real moment, even when the reader already knows the poem well. Such a poem is thus realist and mimetic, in that it becomes a dramatisation of a moment of someone's experience and self-expression, even when that self-expression is highly composed and is contained by the obviously artificial devices of stanza, metre and rhyme. Movement poets believed, in addition, that the familiarity of certain historical poetic forms would provide another bond with the reading public, and appeal to a sense of traditional national identity.

'Confessional' poetry is one genre within this category, marked by intense personal revelation on the part of a character who seems to be the poet speaking directly. Other genres include dramatic monologue in which the speaker is clearly not the poet, and monologue in which the poet seems to speak directly but presents general argument rather than personal confession. All of these are established traditions. But their shared disadvantage is that it is extremely difficult for this kind of mimetic realism to present the large-scale material processes and technical systems that determine much of life but are, for the most part, beyond personal perspective and the language of ordinary people, or whatever can be identified plausibly as a sample of that language.[1]

Among the processes and systems of this kind that appear in *The Oval Window* are human anatomy, computer software and the financial markets. In the technical detail of their operations, these systems lie beyond the kind of knowledge that can be attributed to a personal point of view that can be called typical or broadly representative. They are known by means of specialist expertise, and mostly through the use of technical terminology. A dramatic speaker may be an expert in one of these fields, able to offer explanations, and one can imagine a poetic monologue arising from investigations of one of these subjects carried out by a poet without prior expertise – a monologue giving the poet's personal response. But the more elaborate and technical the explanations need to be, and the greater the number of systems and processes that the poet seeks to acknowledge, the more difficult it will be to combine such explanation with dramatic or lyrical intensity.

Here is another kind of marginalisation of poetry. The literary form that historically has been regarded as the most elevated and transcendent seems to be locked out of any perspective other than the personal, and left barely able to contemplate the most powerful large-scale shaping forces revealed by expert analysis. This is the context in which we should see Prynne's relinquishing

---

1. See, for example, Sam Solnick, *Poetry and the Anthropocene: Ecology, biology and technology in contemporary British and Irish poetry* (London: Routledge, 2016), for a detailed reading of Prynne's references to biochemical science, and for the fullest ecocritical account of Prynne's work to date.

of the personal lyric voice – or, sometimes, as in *The Oval Window*, his interspersing of that voice with impersonal material, so that the voice disappears and re-emerges. Since the 1968 publication of *Kitchen Poems*, the first collection included in the current Bloodaxe *Poems*, a fundamental component of Prynne's poetry has been the use of lines quoted from different sources, literary, scientific and otherwise technical, without the mediation of a dramatic speaker of these lines – though sometimes such a speaker appears in the midst of them. Often the first effect is abrupt and harsh contrast. At times, elements from the different sources seem almost to merge as a single statement, but only momentarily and meltingly.

These lines, passages and fragments are mixed together so that their relations are dialectical. That is to say, the poetic effect consists of the interaction of contrasting and opposing elements that continue to challenge and transform each other. The term 'dialectical' here should not suggest a progression from the encounter with two opposing elements to a single powerful synthesis that resolves their opposition. A look at the particular set of contradictory elements that Prynne assembles reveals such an outcome to be remote. The necessary conditions for such a resolution are clearly not within reach, though the revelation of their remoteness is powerful and admonitory. For example – and it is a central example – Prynne continually challenges the impulse to joyful lyricism with the suspicion that the lyricism and the joy are not innocent. On the contrary, they are complacent; they constitute a turning-away from the work of recognising one's complicity with social injustice and war, and, since that complicity belongs to everyone likely to be reading, the turning-away into lyricism and unearned self-exaltation is a ruse knowingly deployed by all of us and facilitated by poets (sometimes as part of the heritage industry). These are the suspicions and charges that compose the anti-thesis in the dialectic. Technical language of any kind implies deliberate pragmatic manipulation, made possible by the restriction of a piece of language to a single utilitarian sense.

In Prynne's work, this dialectical process, in which each side repeatedly challenges the other, can be seen even in the alternative meanings and intonations of single words and phrases, as we shall see. A sardonically cynical sense challenges an idealistic sense, and is challenged in turn, for neither can stabilize as the final satisfying reading (the suspicious attitude carries its own dangers of complacency). Each needs and provokes the challenge of the other. What sort of synthesis could resolve this opposition? All that is available in present circumstances is synthesis – and song – of the most provisional kind, emerging tentatively and warily in the gaps between thesis and anti-thesis, and always subject to imminent dissolution. A philosophical text to which Prynne responded strongly, as he was developing these poetic strategies in the late 1960s, was Theodor Adorno's *Negative Dialectics*. It seems clear that Prynne saw this work as having affinities with his own concerns. He has recently identified it as a book that has 'meant a lot' to him.[2] Adorno argues that, since no concept is fully identical to the object it describes, and no concept comprehends the full life and meaning of that object, every dialectical synthesis will leave behind a residue that has moral importance and will re-assert itself in some form unless brutally suppressed.[3]

The dialectical exchange continues to the end of the poem, and implicitly beyond it. Prynne's long-term interest in philosophical and political traditions of seeing the world as dialectical process has run alongside his interest in scientific perspectives upon ceaseless material change, from geology to particle physics. In the contrasts between different niches in the culture, and in single words and phrases, a technical sense challenges a colloquial or symbolic sense, a sacred sense challenges a secular sense, and sardonic levity challenges exalted lyricism. These alternatives circle each other, the momentary emergence of one prompting the other to displace it, sometimes instantly. This is an orientation that places great pressure on the poet's need to come to an ending, and the question of how poems can end without suppression of one side of the dialectic has long been foregrounded in Prynne's work. His comic prose poem 'The *Plant Time Manifold* Transcripts', in the 1974 collection *Wound Response*, ends with the observation that 'I stop before I do.'[4]

---

2. Interview in *The Paris Review* 218, Fall 2016, p. 188.

3. Prynne gives a revealing account of dialectical practices of writing and reading in a remarkable commentary upon John Keats's 'Ode on a Grecian Urn', published in *Epsians*, Vol. 4, 2014 (1), pages 49-86. He finds in the poem, at its 'central core', a 'deliberately self-contested theme' (p. 61). 'Everywhere these latent puns carry on a critical or even adverse counter-meaning' (p. 63), so that 'none of the possible resolutions can claim self-evident authority over the alternatives', yet the poem demands to be read 'fully and accurately' (p. 74).

4. J.H. Prynne, *Poems* (Hexham: Bloodaxe Books, 2015), p. 242. For a detailed commentary on this work, see Justin Katko, 'Relativistic Phytosophy', *Glossator* Vol. 2 (2010), pp. 245-295.

Adorno uses the term 'constellation' for an assemblage of contradictory elements in dialectical relation that strongly resists synthesis,[5] but in literary discussion of Modernist poetic forms, a word frequently used is 'collage'.[6] I shall use this latter word here, but it should not be taken to imply any inertness in the relations between the assembled pieces of text. There is always movement, in the confrontation between the values and assumptions represented by the different pieces, in the double-meanings of phrases that have, for example, both a sacred and secular sense, in the many puns that jerk the reader between opposite moods, in the dialectical relationship between lyricism and scepticism, which I will discuss further, and in complex shifts and developments of feeling and implication that are comparable to the turns of thought and feeling in realist poetry described above. In 2008, in a keynote speech at the Second Pearl River International Poetry Conference in Gouangzhou, China, reproduced later in the journal *Textual Practice*, Prynne gave an account of these dialectical relations between different textual elements, describing them as a form of 'poetic thought', an 'activity of thought' residing 'at the level of language practice', for which 'the struggle of the poet to separate from it' is an essential precondition. The 'energies' of this thought 'are dialectical and not extruded from personality or point of view'.[7]

Phrases and sentences break off unfinished, interrupted by others; in this way the vocabularies from different places, carrying their different assumptions, merge and appear in strange juxtapositions. Sometimes a poetic voice finds space for extended lyrical flight, or the disparate elements bind together in passages of lyrical intensity in which the cadences continue while the sense and vocabulary shift. At other times, these vocabularies stand off from each other, with little to bridge the gaps of sense and syntax. The reading process, too, will involve passages of fluency and acceleration followed by dissolution and regrouping.

Some insight into the purposes and effects of this technique may come from

---

5. Theodor Adorno, *Negative Dialectics*, tr. E. B. Ashton (New York: Continuum International, 2007), p. 162.

6. See, for example, Marjorie Perloff, 'Collage and Poetry', in Michael Kelly, ed., *Encyclopedia of Aesthetics*, Vol. 1 (New York: Oxford University Press, 1998), pp. 384-387: http://marjorieperloff.com/essays/collage-poetry/

7. J.H. Prynne, 'Poetic Thought', *Textual Practice* 24 (4), 2010, 595–606, pp. 596, 597.

recent schools of theory. Posthumanism, Actor-Network Theory, Biosemiotics and New Materialism have all sought to extend some of the fundamental propositions of Post-structuralist thought from the linguistic, cultural and psychoanalytical realms to the material world, including the human body recognised as inseparable from the ecosystem that continuously sustains and renews it. These schools of thought converge on the idea that, in perception and representation, a shift of emphasis is required, from the individual subject as protagonist to the larger material systems in which that subject is embedded and by which it is generated — systems extended across space and time. Ecocritical theorist Hannes Bergthaller summarises the shift advocated by New Materialism:

> Its intellectual project is a redescription of the world that dissolves the singular figure of the human subject, distinguished by unique properties (soul, reason, mind, free will or intentionality), into the dense web of material relations in which all things are enmeshed.[8]

For the Material Feminist critic Stacy Alaimo, 'trans-corporeality' is the term that best conveys the idea:

> I argue for a conception of trans-corporeality that traces the material interchanges across human bodies, animal bodies, and the wider material world. As the material self cannot be disentangled from networks that are simultaneously economic, political, cultural, scientific, and substantial, what was once the ostensibly bounded human subject finds herself in a swirling landscape of uncertainty [...] even as global capitalism and the medical-industrial complex reassert a more convenient ideology of solidly bounded, individual consumers and benign, discrete products.[9]

The individual body is constituted by a constant process of exchange and flow, as substances enter it and leave it, and the body itself dissolves and is renewed. Alaimo and Bergthaller call for representations that reveal the body's inseparability from that flow. Feminist philosopher and particle phy-

---

8. Hannes Bergthaller, 'Limits of Agency', in Serenella Iovino & Serpil Oppermann, eds, *Material Ecocriticism* (Bloomington: Indiana University Press, 2014), 37-50, p. 37.

9. Stacy Alaimo, *Exposed: Environmental Politics and Pleasures in Posthuman Times* (Minneapolis: University of Minnesota Press, 2016), p. 112.

sicist Karen Barad proposes the term 'intra-activity' as a general replacement for 'inter-activity', since the implication of the former is that separate pre-formed entities are engaging with each other, whereas the latter term has them already within the same system.

These schools of thought and shifts of emphasis can help us understand Prynne's poetic forms, and also his subject-matter, since there is an analogy running through his work between the form of the poem and the other entities whose boundaries have been made more indistinct by this shift of emphasis from individual to larger flow. One of these entities is the physical human body, with particular emphasis on eyes and ears as thresholds (the Oval Window is an organ in the inner ear with a name that also makes us think of visual perception).[10] Another entity is the individual's sense of selfhood, and another is the building or place that is a home, dwelling or shelter – pre-eminently, in *The Oval Window*, the stone shieling with its window, pictured on the original cover and described shortly before the book's end. These are all points of vantage: positions or platforms from which the wider surroundings – the environment outside – can be observed. They are spaces defined by divisions between inside and outside, and in the poem these divisions and thresholds are successively overwhelmed and re-established, dissolving and tentatively re-forming. This is also true of another entity with melting boundaries but a strong impulse to resist dissolution and draw everything together so as to be able to move on lyrically – the act of reading the poem.

Collage of this kind is clearly a device for breaking boundaries and disrupting cultural niches, so as to bring together discourses normally kept separate (literary, scientific, medical, financial, technological). In *The Oval Window*, there is a paradoxical combination of openness and restriction, the latter revealed by the poem's archive, to which we had access for this edition. The lines and phrases quoted in the poem to make up its collage of found material come from literary sources (especially Shakespeare and *Among the Flowers*, an anthology of translations of ninth- and tenth-century Chinese poems), from a variety of specialist books (especially two works on the anatomy of the eye, and one on computer programming, Kernighan and Plauger's *The Elements of*

---

10. For a more extensive account of the poem's use of references to the snow-like otolith crystals in the inner ear, see N.H. Reeve and Richard Kerridge, *Nearly Too Much: The Poetry of J.H. Prynne* (Liverpool: Liverpool University Press, 1995).

Programming Style) and from newspaper reports and articles on various subjects, especially the financial markets. Of the newspaper quotations, twenty-three out of twenty-five are from the editions of *The Times* and *Financial Times* published between the 22nd and the 30th of August 1983 (the other two are from *The Cambridge Evening News* of September 1st 1983, and *The Times* of 22nd August 1981). That nine-day period – in which, presumably, at least parts of the poem were being written – functions as a snapshot of the multitudinous world with its complex and powerful systems. The short period constitutes a framed window upon that world.

Prynne's turn, in the early 1960s, towards open poetic forms in the Modernist tradition was strongly influenced by American writers in that tradition, in whom he saw a bold alternative to the Movement aesthetic then dominant on the British scene. He has recently described his reaction to Donald Allen's 1960 anthology *The New American Poetry*, one of the most important bringers of new American Modernist work to British audiences:

> It wasn't exactly that the ideas or the arguments registered strongly with me. It was that the energy and innovativeness and newness of outlook, and the experiments with forms, prosodies, rhythms, and matters of present-ation, including the whole mise-en-page, were completely unprecedented in English practise at the time. To break up the presence of the word forms across the page and to distribute them according to rhythm and emphasis was unprecedented in British habit.[11]

One of the most prominent of these American Modernists was Charles Olson, with whom Prynne conducted a fascinating correspondence between 1961 and 1970, the year of the American poet's death.[12] Readers pondering the question of how to read Prynne can find help in the conception of poetic form that Olson expounded in 1950, in his essay 'Projective Verse' (the critic Kathleen Fraser has described the publication of this essay as an 'immense permission-giving moment'[13] for poets seeking to experiment with page-space). Olson

---

11. Interview in *The Paris Review* 218, Fall 2016, p. 180.

12. Recently published as *The Collected Letters of Charles Olson and J.H. Prynne*, ed. by Ryan Dobran (Albuquerque: University of New Mexico Press, 2017).

13. Kathleen Fraser, *Translating the Unspeakable: Poetry and the Innovative Necessity* (Tuscaloosa: University of Alabama Press, 2000), p. 175.

conceives the 'projective' poem as constituting an 'open field', in which objects and quotations appear suddenly, in all their strangeness, without introduction, not contained by the point of view of a narrator-character. The absence of such a persona – and, in the case of collage, the absence of stable, continuous context and linear sense – is a clearing of space around each piece of language, each different kind. Hence the use of the word 'open': the whole world, as it passes by, in all its flowing information, seems to be open to the poem, which can pluck anything from it. This openness also brings about a blurring of the time frame, so that the encounter with each piece of information occurs at the reader's moment, the moment of reading, as much as the implied dramatic moment of writing or speaking. Openness can be temporal as well as spatial. If something in the poem is clearly occurring at a particular moment, then that moment becomes a receding landmark in the reader's open landscape, and there is a sense of the precise distance between that landmark and the moment of reading.

For writers of this kind of poetry, the aspiration is that the poem should not be an enclosing field with hard boundaries. It should not use a dramatic 'point of view' as a restrictive field in which the entities that appear in the poem are contained. These entities should not only appear as perceived by the speaker at a particular dramatic moment or in the context of a particular argument in which they are being used. They should also be encountered in the relatively open context of each reader's life at the moment of reading – open because that reader's sense of surrounding space encompasses the whole earth, its history and its unfolding processes. For this to be possible, the particular dramatic moment of speaking and the subjectivity of the speaker have to be cut out of the poem, or parts of the poem at least. That is one kind of opening up of the poetic space: the removal of a frame.

Another kind occurs when the process of reading is made to expand so that it can accommodate the reader's investigation of unfamiliar terms and the fields that lie behind them, an activity that may be so prolonged and open-ended that it cannot go on uninterrupted. Reading ceases to be a single contained action, insofar as it was ever that. Line by line, the reader has to pause and search for terms and phrases on the internet, or look them up elsewhere, before returning to the poem. Prynne's work requires this continually. Such reading melts into the background of the reader's life, intermitting with other experiences, diffusing, intermingling and – this is the hope – spreading and penetrating further, and interacting more variously.

All of this might be said of any reading experience that profoundly touches the reader, prompting continuing thought and releasing currents of feeling that go on to attach themselves to new experiences. But Prynne produces a kind of writing that refuses to be read any other way. The poem has to take up a disruptive amount of the reader's life if it is to be read at all. Its audacity is in this bid to turn the reader into someone in whose life poetry plays such a large part, if that is not already true. Prynne's poetry defies rapid consumption. It cannot be read quickly and uninterruptedly, except as a beautiful but enigmatic surface, until a great deal of preparation has taken place – so much, that the idea of the eventual, uninterrupted reading turns into a mirage, always ahead.

Sometimes the lyricism carries me forwards when my mind is protesting feebly, 'stop, wait, I need to look something up here'. The poem carries on and is over before I am ready. At other times, a line sends me off to look something up, life intervenes, and a week passes before I go back to the text, still there with the same order and completeness. Prynne is interested in thresholds and spaces that are defined by the flowing in and flowing out of material, but nevertheless provisionally, and sometimes eloquently, hold that material together, fleetingly yet for long enough.

Long enough for what? Prynne's critical writing reveals one answer. His readings of Shakespeare's sonnets and of Wordsworth show his fascination with the role of lyric poetry in Christian and subsequent secular traditions of stoicism and consolation in the face of mortality and mutability. Prynne's poetry is engaged in an unsparing examination of how tenable that tradition remains, and what forms it can take, in our contemporary world of globalised capitalism, information systems and scientific understanding. A vital part of this exploration – this attempt to achieve lyric release and consolation scrupulously, without self-deception, in our present-day circumstances – is a preoccupation with various effects of time, space and cultural niche. How momentary can lyric release be, without becoming so painfully exposed and frail as to lose stoical authority and become merely plaintive? Is the space in which lyric release is possible an enclosed and exclusive space? If so, how compromised and self-deceiving about privilege does the poetry become? Does it offer forms of consolation that live contentedly in protected spaces, averting their eyes from ruthless logics of power and thus co-existing with the prevailing regime much more happily than the poet pretends? These are traditional questions, but Prynne's exploration of them is resolutely contemporary.

A third term joins the analogy between human bodies and poetic forms. What about the practice of reading? What form does that practice take, and what sort of niche, in a life, a culture, a political economy, does the practice occupy? A simple observation about Prynne's work is that it blocks the process of conventional reading, partly through apparent discontinuities of sense and partly through the unmediated use of obscure technical vocabularies. This means that quick uninterrupted reading – what we might call ordinary reading – is frustrated, or perhaps deferred and still hovering before us as an experience that will be possible once certain work has been done: most obviously the work of looking words up and then trying to understand how the contrasting elements fit together.

Obstruction of this kind foils the instant and unreflective gratifications associated with heedless consumerism. Does it also foil, or at least suspend, the possibility of lyric release? Questions are raised about how long reading can reasonably be expected to take, or, from another point of view, how much time the reader must be willing to devote, if the practice is to be serious and conscientious. And what will the reward be at the end? There is an invocation here, sometimes forcefully ironical, of the Christian tradition of transcendent redemptive release as the reward for a long life of faith and serious moral effort. Reading that requires research enacts in miniature this structure of deferment and effort, though there will be frequent alternation between preparatory effort and lyrical release, rather than a single concluding redemption.

That structure is also enacted by the format of the critical commentaries Prynne has published in recent years. These are intensive studies of particular short poems (Shakespeare's 'Sonnet 94', Wordsworth's 'The Solitary Reaper' and George Herbert's 'Love (III)'),[14] which take the form of word-by-word and phrase-by-phrase readings across a hundred pages or so. After a general introduction, each significant word has a section of commentary exploring the relevant conceptual history and various implications and alternative senses. Often, several pages are devoted to a single word. Thus a process of reading is displayed that goes beyond what is conventionally called 'close

---

14. J.H. Prynne, *They that Haue Powre to Hurt: A Specimen of a Commentary on Shake-speares Sonnets, 94* (Cambridge, 2001); J.H. Prynne, *Field Notes: The Solitary Reaper and Others* (Barque Press, 2007); J.H. Prynne, *George Herbert, Love III. A Discursive Commentary* (Barque Press, 2011).

reading', enabling us to glimpse a potentially infinite activity. The readings are full of pauses and digressions: spaces that have been made for deep research and reflection that could clearly go deeper still. It is a method that raises the question of how these extensive findings can feed back into a single fluent reading of the poem. Dissolution threatens. The idea of that single comprehensive reading-experience comes to seem more and more transcendental and redemptive in character: a sort of always-deferred final synthesis that would overcome, among other dichotomies, the division between intellectual and emotional responses. Yet such a reading, in a more provisional sense, is tangibly at hand at all times, since the last page of the volume folds open so that the poem in its short entirety can sit alongside each page of commentary, inviting the eye to flit continually between fragmentation and wholeness.

A sort of compromise is offered by availability of search engines such as Google. These are resources that can also sit at hand as one reads the poem. The search engine is a saver of time and space that makes this sort of extensively researched reading possible for people unable to spend days in a huge library. But this compromise scarcely overturns the contrast between slow and fast reading. On the contrary, it makes the slower version available to ordinary readers (as opposed to professional academic specialists) to a much greater extent than before, and thus sets the dilemma more challengingly. Prynne's work demands a reader who is willing not only to defer the gratification of the complete (or at least provisionally complete) reading experience in one sitting, but also to allow the longer process of interruption and resumption to take up a larger and more dispersed part of their lives. Reading enters, as a result, into different relationships with other activities and priorities. It becomes a different part of the person's identity, and can be seen as a challenge to the values of rapid-consumption consumerism.

With all this in mind, I want to make an experimental beginning of a reading of *The Oval Window*, with search engine at hand, and with the information about the poem's source-materials that the newly available archive provides.

*

Here are the first lines again:

> The shut inch lively as pin grafting
> leads back to the gift shop, at a loss
> for two-ply particles

What can we do with this, to start off our reading? In those first lines, the terms that immediately need looking-up are 'pin grafting' and 'two-ply particles', both clearly technical. 'Two-ply' is also a literary reference, however, for one of the greatest originators of the Modernist collage method in poetry is Ezra Pound's *The Cantos*, and in Canto IV Pound uses the phrase 'Ply over ply' to describe his materials and their relationship.[15] The combination of this phrase with 'particles' suggests that poets using this method may now aspire somehow to involve in their poetic effects the processes of exchange that take place at sub-microscopic scales. Such a perspective, though it is only broached in the smallest way here, would further complicate our perceptions of the relative solidity and separateness of selves. Later we will encounter references to the minutest shifts among the inner ear's otolith crystals.

I enter 'pin grafting' and get a list of sites concerned with state of the art techniques for the grafting of plants in order to accentuate certain desired characteristics of the species that is grafted onto another. This ancient horticultural practice is a precursor to the currently controversial use of genetic modification for the hybridising of organisms, but it too has been at various times a source of anxiety, due to the perception that the artificial violation of species-boundaries – a violation that could not occur by natural breeding of even a guided kind – represents an assumption of a creative role previously reserved to divinity. Dangers of blasphemy and misbegottenness arise. Prynne has a long-standing interest in the contorted implications of grafting as a poetic metaphor, explored particularly in *Graft and Corruption* (2015), a critical pamphlet discussing the history and meaning of the metaphor as used in Shakespeare's 'Sonnet 15' (this booklet does not follow the commentary format previously described).[16]

In the sonnet, the metaphor concerns the claim of the poet that his work can act as consolation for his lover's ageing, mortality and loss of beauty, but behind this secular purpose there is a tradition of using the analogy to describe the relationship between body and soul. Prynne exposes problems in such metaphorical correspondences, due principally to the horticultural fact that it is the scion – the new plant-material grafted onto the rooted plant – that dominates and sets the basic character of the ensuing product. The stock,

---

15. Ezra Pound, *The Cantos* (London: Faber & Faber, 1975), p.15.
16. J.H. Prynne, *Graft and Corruption: Shakespeare's Sonnet 15* (Face Press, 2015).

the initial plant, is a mere holder whose species-characteristics do not survive and develop. Therefore the question of which part represents the body and which the soul is fraught with difficulty, and the metaphor does not work coherently either way.

For readers beginning *The Oval Window*, however, what is most important at this early stage is not any complication of this kind, but simply that we have a technical term that invokes the crossing and modification of species-boundaries and complicates distinctions between self and other and nature and artifice. A theme of the poem is thus introduced, enabling us to back-track and make sense of the very first words. 'Shut inch' carries a suggestion of 'shut in', but leads to the more positive 'lively', giving us an ambivalence about the relationship between confinement and creativity that becomes clearer once the 'shut inch' seems likely to be the pin-shaped scion inserted in the grafting operation.

Already, after three words, the reader may feel shut into the poem, but is asked to accept this condition for the sake of the liveliness that may ensue, though in the next line 'back to the gift shop' adds a note of wryness to this commitment. A gift shop is usually to be found at any leisure-site of potentially ambitious cultural, intellectual, emotional and spiritual interest, such as a museum, historic building, art gallery, zoo, nature reserve or landscape-feature. In such places, the gift shop embodies the simplest kind of commercial commodification of the attraction, and an effortless, reductive form of consumption, as opposed to any more demanding engagement. Often the gift shop is near the entrance of the site. So, to turn straight back to the gift shop almost immediately after arriving is to make an almost comic surrender of purpose. It is already too much for me. I am already 'at a loss', or perhaps already lost in the pathways through the exhibit, which all seem conveniently to lead back to the gift shop. Prynne frequently uses a device of which Samuel Beckett was fond: the incorporation in the dramatic context of phrases one cannot help seeing as sardonic metatextual references to a baffled reader's (or in Beckett's case audience-member's) experience, such as, in Act 1 of *Waiting for Godot*, Estragon's line, 'Nothing happens, nobody comes, nobody goes, it's awful!'[17] In these first lines of *The Oval Window*, there is a comic challenge to the reader in the idea of someone giving up after a few minutes, turning back

---

17. Samuel Beckett, *Waiting for Godot* (London: Faber & Faber, 2010), p. 38.

and settling for the gift shop.[18]

But that is only the opening round of a dialectic between strenuous efforts and 'gift shop' values that develops through the poem, especially in the recurrent image, later on, of the toy snowstorm, with its building, landscape or character enclosed in a plastic dome of liquid, in which white or silver flakes flurry when the toy has been turned upside-down and then righted. This is a typical piece of gift shop merchandise, usually containing a crude plastic model of a building, landscape or character, but in *The Oval Window* this toy has a teasing resemblance to two of the poem's most important objects of attention: the stone shelter, a small redoubt temporarily holding together in a swirling world, and the Oval Window in the inner ear, with its flakes, the otolith crystals, shifting and heaping with the body's movement so as to stabilise the individual's orientation and sensory intake. By visual suggestion, both objects lead to two more. One is the individual self, the bearer of consciousness, capable of action, but mortal, temporary and vulnerable to large-scale catastrophes such as famine ('three to one herring') and war ('in hot sun, blue streak' – Neil Reeve's essay in this volume reveals the meaning of that phrase). The other is the poem itself. It too is a precarious structure amidst the swirl: an entity that draws in material from different directions, fragments from the past and parts of statements caught in mid-flow, and precariously holds these elements together, sometimes loosely and sometimes combining them in urgent or lyrical fluency. These resemblances mean that the gift shop toy does not only function as an undemanding and sentimental substitute for the serious experience, and a sardonic challenge to the reader, but also as a pathway back into the serious territory, as the poem tilts between moods. The whole poem ends with 'a toy hard to bear'.

Further down that first page:

> What can't be helped
> Is the vantage, private and inert; yet
> in a twinkling mind you, to pick up
> elastic replacements on the bench code.

---

18. For a discussion of some more general significances of the idea of 'the gift' in Prynne's work, see Rod Mengham, '"A Free Hand to Refuse Everything": Politics and Intricacy in the Work of J.H. Prynne', in Ian Brinton, ed., *A Manner of Utterance: The Poetry of J.H. Prynne* (Exeter: Shearsman Books, 2009), pp. 69-82.

'Can't be helped', meaning 'can't be avoided, though I would like to' ('I can't help it'), or 'can't be helped' meaning doomed beyond salvation, beyond help? The double meaning expresses the ambivalence about literary point of view and the individual's sense of bounded selfhood discussed earlier – the ambivalence that runs through the poem. For 'vantage', as in 'point of vantage', means a relatively stable and detached position from which a stretch of land can be observed. The vestigial stone shelter still has the capacity to provide one, and one is also provided and framed by the oval shape of the eyelids, and the Oval Window in the ear. Famous points of vantage in poetic history include the elevated viewpoint of William Wordsworth's protagonist in 'Lines Composed A Few Miles Above Tintern Abbey', a Romantic adaptation of the eighteenth-century genre called the 'Prospect Poem', in which the speaker characteristically surveys a wide space from high ground, and is moved to reflection on long time-perspectives also. In *The Oval Window*, the crumbling stone shelter has a Wordsworthian aura, and the poem presents a running dialectic between positions down in the midst of the swirling language and positions of elevated viewpoint. If the reader attempts to chase, through research, the precise meaning of a technical phrase, they are embroiled in the midst and up close to the language, whereas if they are content to identify language by general type, they are retreating to a more distant point of observation.

When I searched for 'elastic replacements', a range of products and contexts came up, including garden furniture and nappies, but the phrase does not appear to be a precise technical term. Its general sense is clear. This phrase and 'bench code' evoke DIY or the servicing of domestic appliances, while also sounding as if they might come from the jargon of information technology. 'Bench code' brings these two worlds together, and my search for that phrase took me to 'bench coding', a term for the construction of virtual environments in which software is tested.

To repair the failing vantage, then, if it has become too private and inert, we can apparently 'pick up elastic replacements'. The trace of an advertiser's voice enters here. Prynne regularly counterpoints lyrical passages and collage with this sort of ironic cynicism. As with the mention of the gift shop, the teasing suggestion here is that the 'vantage', in all the senses identified above, can be seen as an appliance, available in shops near you. Rather than a viewpoint and sensibility arising naturally and guilelessly, or a place of outlook attained through effort and courage, the 'vantage' might be a purchased product for which replacement parts can easily be obtained.

Similarly, 'set callow', earlier on the same page, sounds like a technical term (though my internet search did not find it), but when applied to the poem can give us the cynical thought that trusting innocence, as a state of mind belonging to writer or reader, might be a 'setting', a point to which a dial can be deliberately turned. A couple of lines later, 'block for scatter' prompts an internet search that leads to acoustics, since scatter blocks are wall-panels installed to produce sonic environments in which some sounds are eliminated and others magnified while the overall ambience seems natural. I found several adverts for these.

Naturally, any perceiving organism has evolved so as to orient itself in the world by receiving some signals and not others. Complete openness would be overwhelming. But there is a troubling suggestion here that what seems to be a spontaneous and unguarded encounter in the poem's 'open field' might really be a much more calculated and controlled effect. Could the apparently open field be in reality a precisely but invisibly regulated environment? More-over, it is possible that the person having the encounter – the poet-protagonist and the reader alike – might not want to see this. They might want to protect their illusion of innocence and courageous exposure, leaving the protections to be provided invisibly by specialists such as acoustics engineers. Such a tacit and unacknowledged wish requires that the language of poetry be kept separate from the technical language of the expert protectors, and that the latter should be opaque.

How is that bad faith to be avoided? The challenge these suggestions make to the reader is that, although we should give ourselves up to each textual moment, feeling the emotional release that comes when dialectical complexities are drawn up into a lyrical wave, we must also try to see the place of the vantage-point in the larger cultural and economic systems invoked by the poem. That is in any case what the collage method presses us to do. It is why the poem must include the technical vocabulary, requiring the reader to invest-igate each term's meaning. On the first page of the poem, we have glancing references to horticultural grafting, surgical grafting, the concealed manipul-ation of acoustics, and the extension of human observation by means of com-puter technology. All of these are deliberate creative and manipulative disrup-tions of the natural boundaries of entities, revealing the larger systems and processes in which those entities take place and by which they are formed. A lyricism, expressive of joy in the outlook at a particular moment, can only avoid the bad faith if it emerges from an awareness of these systems, as expansiveness and as limitation. A similar doubleness occurs on the next page, in the lines:

> Smartly clad they could only panic
> through the medium itself

These words will be repeated later in the poem. Should we read them as saying that all 'they' could do was panic, running frantically through the full extent of all the linguistic and cultural signs to hand, and sending a shock through the whole system? Or should we interpret the lines as saying that even such a supposedly disruptive force as panic, with its buried reference to Pan, will have no form of expression but those social and linguistic signs, which will contain the panic; it will not break out or change them. 'Only *panic* through the medium' or 'only panic through the *medium*'? 'Smartly clad' is suggestive of weapons systems, as is 'smart guidance' a line later, but the archive reveals the source of 'Smartly clad' to be a description in *The Times* of the clothes worn by the band ZZ Top at a concert. The innocent and the ominous meanings constantly displace each other.

Another paradox is brought by the word 'twinkling'. 'In a twinkling mind you', says the advertiser's jolly tone, persuading us to accept the position of a child being promised a treat (the absence of a comma after 'twinkling' also gives us the suggestion of a 'twinkling mind' whose thought-processes are dazzlingly rapid). The sources of this phrase, as revealed by the archive, are surprising, in that they are far removed from this childish and domestic aura. Indeed, they are at the opposite end of the scale: apocalyptic and visionary. In the King James Bible, I Corinthians 15, 51-52, gives us, 'Behold, I shew you a mystery; We shall not all sleep, but we shall all be changed. / In a moment, in the twinkling of an eye, at the last trump'. A second source is a line from the first English translation, in the 1950s, of the *Wen fu*, the classic essay on poetic composition by the third-century Chinese poet and critic Lu Ji. Of the poet who has 'mustered what for a hundred generations awaited his pen', the essay says:

> Eternity he sees in a twinkling,
> And the whole world he views in one glance.

In each source, the largest amount of space and time ('we shall all', 'eternity', 'the whole world') is abruptly collapsed into the smallest, the twinkling of an eye. The apocalyptic meanings hiding in the phrase are only revealed at this stage of reading if the reader is aware of the biblical source. Later, they may be released by the reference to Blue Streak, and the various evocations of war and of moments just before death. On this first page, however, what is more likely to be striking is the condescension in the advertiser's use of a presumably childish word, and behind the advertiser the poet's sardonic challenge. For the reader at this point, the most immediate association of the word 'twinkling' is likely to be with 'Twinkle, twinkle, little star'. In 1992, nine years after *The Oval Window*, Prynne included in one of his William Matthews Lectures, given at Birkbeck College, what he called a 'playful over-reading'[19] of this nursery rhyme. His concern was with the relationship between immediate domestic surroundings and vast distances. The rhyme is reassuring to childish ears because it brings a vast context into scale with what the child recognises:

> The vast scale and remoteness of phenomena are potentially frightening, as also the imminent loneliness at bed-time; but each word reduces this scale to the friendly and protective charm of little things. Because of the pattern, and within the discourse context of adult language-use directed at a childish audience, one order, that of sound, leads by invitation onto another order, that of sense, pointing it up while scaling it down.

Potentially, the scale-effect goes the other way too. Cosmic entities have been scaled down so as to become toys in the nursery, but once brought within those walls they can be scaled up again, and contemplated in their vastness.[20]

---

19. J.H. Prynne, Stars, *Tigers and the Shape of Words* (© J.H. Prynne, 1993), p. 10.

20. A combination of expansive and diminutive pressure around the word 'toy', in some ways similar, is to be found in Coleridge's 'Frost at Midnight', a poem on which Prynne has lectured and that he clearly loves. A film of soot (known as a 'stranger') fluttering in the grate of the poet's fire becomes a kind of Aeolian harp, drawing the poet's mind into new territory in which the imagination is afforded some protection – or given some permission - by the secure homeliness of the setting:

> Still flutters there, the sole unquiet thing.
> Methinks, its motion in this hush of nature
> Gives it dim sympathies with me who live,
> Making it a companionable form,
> Whose puny flaps and freaks the idling Spirit
> By its own moods interprets, every where
> Echo or mirror seeking of itself,
> And makes a toy of Thought.

This is why the sardonic voice does not have the final word. It is why the vantage-point dissolves and re-forms as the poem goes on; the elastic replacements are a poetic idea as well as a diminutive. And it is why this most famously complex and difficult of writers often wants to contemplate simple short lyrics and songs, or even nursery rhymes.

Another dialectical relationship is produced by the frequent appearance in the later pages of *The Oval Window* of lines from *Among the Flowers*, Lois Fusek's translation of Chao Ch'ung-tso's tenth-century anthology of Chinese *tz'u* poetry.[21] Fusek's introduction explains that *tz'u* lyrics were written to fit the melodies of popular songs, in some cases ancient songs surviving only in this form, the melody having been lost. The lyrics in this anthology were written by court poets at the provincial capital of Szechuan, during and after the collapse of the T'ang dynasty. It was a time of war and widespread social breakdown, but these highly conventional lyrics mostly adopt familiar love-story scenarios, and features from nature so formulaic that they could be on the decorative screens that are also mentioned frequently. Violence and political turmoil register only occasionally, and then only by means of allusions to conflicts that took place hundreds of years earlier, which are invoked by images just as formulaic as the nature-imagery. In many of the poems, the implied speaker-protagonist is a courtesan or 'singing-girl' expressing her longing for an absent lover. These women are the 'flowers' of the anthology's title.

'Implied' is an important word here, for these conventional characters, situations and landscape-features are metonymic allusions to long-established traditions of poetry. No explanation of the protagonist's identity is necessary; the familiar details will tell the reader, and the poem can go straight into the intimacy of the moment without having to introduce anything or lead the reader in. In 1982, the year before *The Oval Window*, Prynne published an enthusiastic account of this method of invoking a traditional genre metonymically. His essay accompanied Anne Birrell's translation of a sixth-century Chinese anthology, *New Songs from a Jade Terrace*. Of the stylised images from nature in that collection, he says:

> The tendency towards a deliberately metonymic system is also thus explicitly opposed to landscape poetry, if by that is meant the un-

---

21. *Among the Flowers: The Hua-chien chi*, tr. Lois Fusek (New York: Columbia University Press, 1982).

mediated associative contemplation of natural objects and perspectives
through a heightened personal perception. [...] [L]andscape here is not
so much a source of images for contemplation as rather a set of tropes for
the separation of lovers by the hardships of distant travel.[22]

This metonymic method is at the opposite end of the spectrum from
'Open Field' poetry. The landscape features and other objects and details that
appear in these stylised love poems are not, like the entities encountered in an
'open field', relatively free from embeddedness in a speaker's prior train of
thought, or any other precise and pre-emptive code. On the contrary, what
they can mean is severely restricted and entirely predetermined by the
traditional code that they invoke. This is not to say that their meaning cannot
be intense, surprising and piercing. In Prynne's account, what is gained by
this method is an extraordinary intensity that comes, for those who know
how to read the code, from the compression of meaning (often erotic
meaning) into slight variations upon established models:

> The extreme reduction and ellipsis of this form only heighten the
> pressure on the resources of nuance and implication, as if constraining all
> the previous tradition to culminate in a set of brilliant needle-points. [...]
> By now the reader has been trained, by the anthologist and his
> translator, in how to read such a deceptively bland-looking fragment.[23]

But in *The Oval Window*, Prynne takes lines and phrases from *Among the
Flowers*, especially nature-images, out of the context in which this metonymic
relationship with their tradition can operate, and intersperses them with his
other material:

> bright moonlight whitens the pear blossom
>
> calm waves flow onward to the horizon
>
> Chill shadows fall from the topmost eaves,

---

22. J.H. Prynne, 'China Figures', in Anne Birrell, tr. *New Songs from a Jade Terrace:
an Anthology of Early Chinese Love Poetry* (Harmondsworth: Penguin Classics, 1986),
p. 374.
23. J.H. Prynne, 'China Figures', p. 389.

clear waters run beside the blossoming peach

A pale white light
from the east is shining in the window

a flowering spray in the glow of the mirror

a mist of gold leaf lightly shimmers
as floating clouds go back to the mountains

Mountains reach across the folds of the screen

The clouds are white in a pale autumn sky.
Looking at the misty paths

A light wind crosses the fragrant waters

dew-drenched apricot flowers

Pear blossoms drift through this garden

she watches for his return
face and flower shining each upon the other

The effect of the extrication of such lines from their metonymic context, and of their insertion into the collage, is to set up a dialectical exchange between the two ends of the spectrum, the two ways of reading. Mixed together, the two modes reveal and define each other, each continually reminding the reader of an alternative approach. Sometimes the dividing-line is unclear:

There
is a snow-down on that sand hillock,
the stars are snowing, do you see it there:
bright moonlight whitens the pear blossom.
You listen out by the oval window, as
calm waves flow onward to the horizon.

Except that sand does not seem right for the shieling's landscape, the first lines here might be direct observation from the oval window in the stone building, though in fact they are taken from Wyndham Lewis's *Enemy of the*

Stars. 'Snow-down' and 'snowing' remind us of the otolith crystals in the Oval Window in the ear, linked throughout the poem to images of snow from a variety of contexts, real and artificial, including the toy snowstorm. A line later, an oval window is mentioned; it might be either the hut or the ear, and is both. In between, the line about pear blossom from *Among the Flowers* clearly does not give us direct observation of the upland landscape, but, nevertheless, the line, in its sensuousness, is integrated into what feels like a single statement registering these different kinds of perception simultaneously. The conventional image is pulled a little way in the direction of realism. Something similar occurs when, a few pages later, 'Calm is all nature as a resting wheel', sandwiched between Chinese fragments, looks as if it too might come from a Chinese source but is in fact from Wordsworth's 'Sonnet: Written in Very Early Youth'. The different kinds of meaning begin to over-lap, and sometimes the proximity is such that the dividing-line is unclear, and we can read a phrase first in one way and then in the other.

*

Throughout this essay I have imagined a reader who has already read *The Oval Window* at least once, and is now moving between the poem and our two essays, comparing. This may or may not be the case. Before this last short passage of my essay, however, I want to do all that is in my power to insist that these thoughts about the last page of *The Oval Window* are addressed to readers who have already encountered that page at the culmination of their first reading of the whole work.

The remarkable, moving eloquence of those final lines is produced, in part, by their relation to what has happened earlier. After so much diffusion, the meanings and dialectical processes now seem contract, or perhaps swoop, into a single dramatic moment, an experience in real time, which is not then expanded from inside, back into open field, as has happened several times before. Early in the poem, with the word 'twinkling', we encountered the idea of vast distance being crossed in a split-second, and eternity being revealed in an instant (the Chinese source revealed by the archive makes this latter idea explicit). Two far extremes are brought together and made to accommodate each other. The idea is apocalyptic, as the biblical source reveals and also in a present-day secular sense, invoking a nuclear war that would end human history in seconds. There is also a suggestion of another

30

development leading us into a post-human world: the capacity of computers to process and survey unimaginable quantities of information in an instant. It is not only children who are in need of reassuring words. 'Twinkling', like many of the characteristic jokes and shifts of register, moves in an instant from seriousness to lightness of tone: another dramatic switch between extremes.

Such extremes are beyond, or at the edge of, human physical observation and the capacities that traditionally define us as human and as selves. But here, at the end of the poem, there is a return to the scale of ordinary dramatic subjectivity in place and time. The protagonist experienced something: 'Standing by the window I heard it, / while waiting for the turn'. Again, the window has several meanings. It is the stone window of the shieling, with all that this building has come to represent symbolically. It is the threshold of the body, at which the subject 'stands' to gaze at or listen to the processes that surround and constitute the body and reach far beyond. It is the particular upland place, as vantage-point, and also the particular moment in time – a moment of precious shelter and poised stillness, however brief, however 'needle-point' and subliminal, the real experience may have been. Perhaps the experience was *extremely* brief, since the perception involved the minutiae of tremors among the otolith crystals, too sub-instantaneous for conscious rationalisation. But it was also a sense of deep, continuous, all-encompassing music, 'the crossing flow of even life', unbounded. Part of the lyrical intensity is this sense of different scales and levels combining, as the line simultaneously registers them all. But the dialectical exchange is still operating. We find it in the different possible senses of the word 'even', which might suggest a resolution in which each side of the dialectic has been given its due: they are even with each other, in the sense of a transaction completed or a grievance compensated, and therefore the ground is even, since neither side presents any longer a craggy forbidding obstacle, and the speaker has thus reached a ridge or summit (the fold line) from which it is possible to descend either way: 'Free / to leave at either side'. But there is another sense of the word 'even', subdued but stubbornly present, in which the word signifies the ut-most that can be achieved, the tenuous far extent of the reach, as in 'I can even do this,' suggesting that this position, this outlook, cannot be held for long.

There is a sense of exposure about these lines, suggestive of that Romantic stance of contemplation of the infinite, and of a precious moment in the lee of impending fate ('while waiting for the turn'). What is 'the turn'? Any abrupt turn in a person's fate, perhaps, since another vantage-point with a window is the single human life, situated in space and time, a platform from which larger and smaller scales can be glimpsed, if the self is not too fearful. There is also a sense of turning seasons. Several times earlier in the poem – especially in the section beginning with 'At the onset of the single life' – that time-frame or platform has been introduced, but it has quickly become trans-corporeal and dissolved into the collage-surroundings. Now there is no time left for such expansion and dissolution. The poem's end is in sight, literally, and the lyric has an urgency that comes from a sense that something needs to be said, while there is still time, but also that something at last *can* be said. 'Joy at death itself' suggests that mortality is the intense concern; it could be joy felt, against the odds, at the moment of death or at the future prospect. 'A toy hard to bear', with its link to the snowstorm and thus to the otolith crystals, suggests a secular poem in the tradition of stoical renunciation that has always fascinated Prynne – so that the ending represents a moment of having won through to the position of genuinely holding life as but a trifle, a toy, without this attitude being a bitter, diminutive rejection of life's infinite interest.

A strong sense of transcendence through renunciation comes also with 'The years / jostle and burn up as a trust plasma', which seems to place the protagonist in an elevated position looking down at his or her own life, or back further at epochs. The line carries a hint of apocalyptic burning, and might be a glancing reference to the possibility of a nuclear missile exchange that would burn up human history in an instant. But then there is the 'trust' in 'trust plasma'. Here, very likely, comes the last recourse to the internet search, which immediately identifies plasma as the most common state of matter in the universe, before offering links associated with the medical transfusion of blood plasma. It was in 2004 that hospitals in the UK began to be called 'trusts', which adds a neat retrospective sharpness to the line's meaning. For readers now – British readers at least – a further irony becomes possible, a jolt into the sardonic attitude. Are we still in a sheltered space, protecting our hopeful sense of the word 'trust', and our belief in our own innocence, from the more cynical uses that abound? 'Trust' has a technical sense in the financial and insurance industries, where the phrase 'single life' is also deployed.

Even in this last lyrical ascent, the poem will not let us forget such questions. But neither will they take up all the space. A better, undeceived and personal sense of trust carries the lyric and carries the mortal protagonist, who is able to see in a spirit of visionary generosity the trans-corporeality of bodies and selves, emerging from larger material processes and dissolving back into them. The response is joy, and a laughter that may be a last utterance that has to reverberate through eternity, but is not finally sardonic.

RICHARD KERRIDGE

THE OVAL WINDOW

(1983)

BEFORE *is* a relation, of degree two, but it is a relation for which not all the underlying domains are *simple*. AFTER is a semantically equivalent relation of degree three, with the property that all its domains *are* simple—in other words, AFTER is normalized.

This condition says essentially that, given the present, the past and future are independent of each other.

The shut inch lively as pin grafting
leads back to the gift shop, at a loss
for two-ply particles
                        set callow,
set bland and clean, wailing as when
to wait is block for scatter. Ah so,
the estrangement of the cause brings off
a surcease of the affect, even end-up
battered in sawdust. You cut your chin
on all this, like club members on the dot
by a winter blaze.
                        What can't be helped
is the vantage, private and inert; yet
in a twinkling mind you, to pick up
elastic replacements on the bench code.

Formerly in a proper tonic, the rain
would pelt and cure by the foam inlet.
    Smartly clad they could only panic
    through the medium itself, rabbit by proxy.
On both sides smart guidance *ex* stock
makes for home like a cup cake over.
          Don't stare:
          Police aware:
it is a defect coma, and it shows;
try it on, see if they'd want to care.

Just a treat sod Heine you notice
the base going down, try to whistle
with a tooth broken. Safe in our hands
won't cut up rough, at all, pent up
and boil over. Fly my brother, he watches
at point of entry, only seeming to
have a heart for it. Thermal patchwork
will tell, sisal entreaty creams out.

Coming through with your back turned
you'd never credit the trick aperture
in part-supply. Being asked to cut
into the bone matches wishing to become
the one that asks and is sharply hurt.
To be controlled as a matter of urgency:
don't turn, it's plasma leaking
               a tune on Monday
               a renewed drive
               not doing enough
to reduce the skin on a grape; the whole
falling short is wounded vantage in
               talk of the town.

Low in these windows you let forth
a lifelong transfusion, as by the selfsame
                hand that made these wounds.
Keep back from the upper notch, running below
a steep flurry of pollen like a pestilence
                rated up for coverage.
The two main shadows over the future tense
are pity and the lack of it, win or lose:
banking on form, the bright lozenge marks
rape swathing under a bandaged sleeve.
Stacking the calls as they come in to land
        a perdita d'occhio the drill rigs
        make a ring of fire, welded on.

Somewhere else in the market it's called
a downward sell-out, to get there first
and cut open a fire break. Less won't do,
more isn't on either. How a gang of boys
set her face alight with a flaming aerosol can,
"her mouth was sealed up by the burns."
Attention is low in historic terms and will
drift down, seeming to falter slowly and
making excuses for the money numbers ahead.

It is deep cold, high cloud on the grill
to hear the swish of a month overhead
in snow on the bush, bird in the hand.
The notice is not lit by cycle time,
blinded to limit the revenant by overt
loss of balance. "He takes pity with him
and makes it possible for him to enter the sea"
with the reflex of naked armour, unplayed
under the lintel.
                The vantage stops off
in arc-light at frosted glass, yet all is shaded
and clumsily mobile. Lately poor eyes.

What if the outlook is likely to cut short
by an inspired fear in the bond market.
The place itself is a birthday prank:
           current past the front,
          en première ligne
like stone dust on strips of brighter green.
Given to allergic twitching, the frame
compounds for invertible counterpoint
and waits to see. A view is a window
on the real data, not a separate copy
of that data, or a lower surplus in oil
and erratic items such as precious stones,
aircraft and the corpses of men, tigers
fish and pythons, "all in a confused tangle."
          Changes to the real data
are visible through the view; and operations
against the view are converted, through
a kind of unofficial window on Treasury policy,
into operations on the real data.
To this world given over, now safely,
work makes free logic joined to the afterlife.

So they burned their boats, looking on
as the frontage went up and footlights
blinked in the watercourse. From each
throat at its fan opening they spoke out
their force of numbers. Either a point
    object or its image point is said
      to be real when the light propagates
through it by ash bluff to printed charcoal.
Count back the poll capture, fun running
like paint from blue to blue over
in the funnel head (sad despair, &c).

Sideways in the mirror and too slow
to take up, it is the point of death. Not
lost from the track as passing its peak
but the cycle burns out on the axle,
quenching a thirst with lip salve slicked
on the ridge of its porridge bowl. Still
spoilt by bad temper the screen relives
a guessed anxiety: wounds were his feast,
his life to life a prey.
                              The internal view
assumes an infinite linear address space,
a table on which are laid out all
the rival manuals of self-sufficiency.
Spring up, O well; sing unto it: but
the answer is a pool of values in prime
hock to a pump and its trade-offs.
That's putting it mildly, by repute.

Do be serious they say, all the time
in the world mounts a deficit
of choice moments fluffed and spilled.
Is misery worse than not knowing its cause,
the wrong fuel in a spirit lamp? The case
rests on tarmac already crumbled
in a pre-recorded dawn chorus:
                    when the furniture was removed
he pulled out the window frames, threw down
the roof, and pushed in the walls. Yet short-
winded the pay-bed recycles a bad debt
as if nothing else counted, as if there are
two distinct and mutually exclusive actions
depending on one test. *Viz*, oilseed
is a fashion laid out like data, the view
loops round from the test drill sponsor
like a bird on the wing. Think now
or pay now and think later, the levels
of control nesting presume a reason
to cut back only and keep mum.

So what you do is enslaved non-stop
to perdition of sense by leakage
                    into the cycle: one man's meat
better late than never. Motor life says
the branch office, a picture is not a window.
In a recursive procedure, the method
of solution is defined in terms of itself; as,
within the chain-guard, cold is the meaning
of heat notably absent. The arctic tern
stays put wakefully, each following suit
by check according to rote; it's precious little,
only smoke damage where that came from.

As what next if you can't, silent fire
dumped in a skip and sun boiling over
the sack race. Best before too late, with
loath to depart in the buff envelope torn across.
I'm finger-perfect by the yard, not like
the ancient sponges putting in question
another glad hand from the puppet dictator.
From the skip there is honey and bent metal,
romantic on trade plates: PUT SKIP EDIT,
PUT SKIP DATA, the control flow structure
demands a check that subscripts do not exceed
array dimensions. That is the regimen,
the bin liner of the second subject, holding
our tongues like brevet clients on call.

Within the frame the match-play is staggered,
to protect the list from its first mistake.
Skip and slip are the antinomian free gifts
mounted on angle-iron reflexes, as sick pay
predates a check to recovery. You're flat out?
But the method sorts downward, wired up
from the NCR cashpoint; you must choose the order
of choice, on the nail from which shadows hang.
What else null else just else if before
out into the garden with overshoot, the
moon is bright as snowy day. In broad
strip neon it ranks as a perfect crime.

In the margin tinted love breaks off
to spot bravura by scrub wintergreen.
Ill met on this road, by invitation
they do keep up while in keeping and
sly good humour. Or sit and choke or
die too, you must mind only so much,
looping ahead with do and while and
calling softly like a fish. Test and store
alla buona, failing to respond, a
sweet smile intent with the marker
in default values; slowness of gaze
goes down with you, flickering to meet
in both the turn for good.

Droplock to gab

by wed foot

fur on the gate

and if flatter so

off you steel

and fall under

Tivoli Tivoli

the better to win

O spite reserve

bred sodden

pad out, fill in

my mitten's

at all given to

hold this piece

forth with and

to the lammas

red

so on go on

of forbidden let

ground

At the onset of the single life
it is joined commonly to what
                    is untasted, lettered out
along the oval window's rim.

And casting the eave forward, in
the first delivery you do know
                    this talc in breath,
marking the helm wind as it cools.

It fans the rim on the inside
of the purlin itself, the tenon gives back
                    exactly your life task
and for the trained level. Grind up

to the hatchment there, they are later
as to the perfect clank. No time
                    first-round, first leg, with
dearer love he too could only panic

through the medium. Hold your chin
to the relief coach; I am a woodland fellow,
                    sirloin parted formerly
that always loved a great fire.

The window glints now in the lee wave,
fed with light up-ended. Crape put out
                    on the hives. Life cover
streams under, the master I speak of

ever keeps a good fire. Give a low
whistle, such country cannot be burnt;
                    fit the rebate, but
sure, he is the prince of the world.

We will cast on the half then and find out
the neural crest below, an inquest
                    wrought with frost without
snow-marking on the run to try

the spoil and waste in a white suit.
Speak truly along the lip there, let
              his nobility remain in's
court. I am for the house again

and the egg-timer, give the sweet air
back as nipped by the bud of ruin:
              three to one herring.
Arms in sisal with the narrow gate

over-arched, knocking at the septum,
which I take to be too little for pomp
              to enter a pleasant fee,
their faces are part-eaten. This is the place

where, deaf to meaning, the life stands
out in extra blue. Some that humble
              themselves at the songbook
may turn the page enchanted; but

the many will be too chill below
in profile, and tender-limbed
              in the foil wrap.
They'll be for the flow'ry way and draw

a sharp breath by flutter action, do it
quickly, tongue tied. That leads
              to the broad gate
and the great fire, and deaf to the face

soundlessly matched to the summit.
We go over. The dip stands down
              in the oval window, in
the blackened gutter stop of the newly born.

As they parted, she heard his horse cry out,
by the rustic lodge in a flurry of snow.
A child's joy, a toy with a snowstorm,
flakes settling in white prisms, to slide
to a stop. The flask is without frame,
metaldehyde safe in cold store. There
is a snow-down on that sand hillock,
the stars are snowing, do you see it there:
bright moonlight whitens the pear blossom.
You listen out by the oval window, as
calm waves flow onward to the horizon.

Her wrists shine white like the frosted snow;
they call each other to the south stream.
The oval window is closed in life,
by the foot-piece of the stapes. Chill shadows
fall from the topmost eaves, clear waters
run beside the blossoming peach. Inside
this window is the perilymph of the vestibule.
     Now O now I needs must part,
      parting though I absent mourne.
It is a child's toy, shaken back in
myopic eddies by the slanting bridge:
toxic; dangerous fire risk; bright moonlight
floods the steps like a cascade of water.

Snow-blinded, we hold our breath;
the echo trembles like a pinpoint, on
each line of the hooded screen. It is life
at the rim of itself, in face of the brow
closed to sorrow. A pale white light
from the east is shining in the window,
a flowering spray in the glow of the mirror.
The internal view burns at this frame,
eyes frozen by calm. For full paralysis
of accommodation, three or four drops
should be instilled every fifteen minutes
for one or two hours. For the rest of
your life. Sight wherein my joys do lie
on a pillow white with shade, brushed
in azure along the folding screen;
all day long, the red door is closed.

So: from now on too, or soon lost,
the voice you hear is your own
revoked, on a relative cyclical downturn
imaged in latent narrow-angle glaucoma.
Yet the snow picks up and infolds,
a mist of gold leaf lightly shimmers
as floating clouds go back to the mountains.
It is not quite a cabin, but (in local speech)
a *shield*, in the elbow of upland water,
the sod roof almost gone but just under
its scar a rough opening: it is, in first
sight, the oval window. Last light foams
at this crest. The air lock goes cold
    in hot sun, blue streak under
lines swarming there, dung on all fours.
The blur spot on both sides gives out
a low, intense hum, sharp-folded as
if to a feral rafter;
               the field is determined
by the *exit window*, the lens rim or stop
which, imaged into image space, subtends
the smallest angle at the centre.
                 So small
here that the pin is bonelike and watched
with the backflood at steep echo,
in brown water clamped at vantage.
Mountains reach across the folds of the screen;
green sedges line the path below cold mist
yet the stone step is boiling fast.
        Upon that dropping floor
        when hope is gone, the sky
        spoken like a roc's egg
in cascaded magnification, runs in
and out and over: honey in snow.

The clouds are white in a pale autumn sky.
Looking at the misty paths I see this stooping
figure seeming to falter, in a thick compound
of adjustments, sublimed in white flakes. Then
it clears down, she turns or round her
the sweet breath goes about, at midnight
murmuring. Extremities flexed and cold.
A light wind crosses the fragrant waters;
deaf to reason I cup my hands, to
dew-drenched apricot flowers and their
livid tranquillity. It has the merit
of being seen to hurt, in her dream,
and then much further on, it does.

Drawn to the window and beyond it,
by the heartfelt screen of a machine
tenderly lit sideways, the wish to enter
the sea itself leaves snow dark as sand.
Pear blossoms drift through this garden,
across the watcher's vantage clouded
by smoke from inside the hut. Tunnel
vision as she watches for his return,
face and flower shining each upon the other.
    So these did turn, return, advance,
      drawn back by doubt, put on by love.
Sort and merge, there is burning along
this frame; and now before you see
you must, we need its name.

It is a CNS depressant. Endless sorrow
rises from the misty waves, like a wick
in the light of conscience. Not feudal
nor slave-owning but the asiatic mode
as locally communal within a despotic state:
the slant of *imperium* coming sideways
"through the competitive examination (*chin-shih*) on Confucian literature." Either contract
or fancy, each framing the other, closed
in life. A flickering lamp burns dimly
at the window, ready for snuff brilliance
which lights the mirror and shades the door.

Now the willows on the river are hazy like mist
and the end is hazy like the meaning
which bridges its frozen banks. In the field
of view a prismatic blur adds on
rainbow skirts to the outer leaves.
   They appropriated not the primary
conditions of labour but their results;
   the waters of spring cross under
the bridge, willow branches dip.
   The denial of feudalism in China
always leads to political errors, of an
essentially Trotskyist order:
   Calm is all nature as a resting wheel.
The red candle flame shakes.

In darkness by day we must press on,
giddy at the tilt of a negative crystal.
The toy is childish, almost below speech
lip-read by swaying lamps. It is not
so hard to know as it is to do:
wresting the screen before the eyelet lost
to speech tune you blame the victim.
Pity me! These petals, crimson and pink,
are cheque stubs, spilling chalk in a mist
of soft azure. At the last we want
unit costs plus VAT, patient grading:
made to order, made to care, poised
at the nub of avid sugar soap.

Standing by the window I heard it,
while waiting for the turn. In hot light
and chill air it was the crossing flow
of even life, hurt in the mouth but
exhausted with passion and joy. Free
to leave at either side, at the fold line
found in threats like herbage, the watch
is fearful and promised before. The years
jostle and burn up as a trust plasma.
Beyond help it is joy at death itself:
a toy hard to bear, laughing all night.

PHOTOGRAPHS

1. Moorland view from Tinkler Crags site.

2. Tinkler Crags.

3. Fir plantation with upland beyond, looking towards MOD land.

4. Wall with spoil heap, stream and fir plantation looking west.

5. Poorly preserved hut remains beside stream.

6. Hut remains showing ground plan.

7. View of King Water with sheepfold and hut site from south.

8. View of sheepfold, with hut wall behind, looking north towards Tinkler Crags.

9. View of wall with window and upland beyond from south.

10. Overgrown doorway showing wooden supports, looking towards fir plantation.

11. Doorway opening in hut wall.

12. Oval Window from south, showing gate and barbed wire from sheepfold.

13. View through window from south, towards Tinkler Crags.

14. View of valley through Oval Window from south.

15. Oval Window from south. The original 1983 cover was a reverse of this image.

16. Oval Window from north, showing corrugated roof over stock shelter.

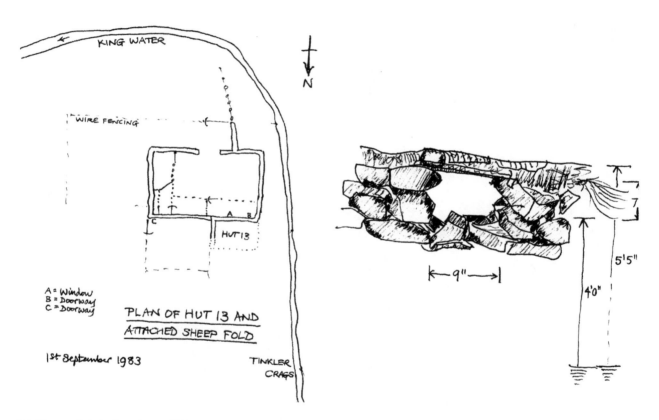

KING WATER

↓
N

WIRE FENCING

HUT 13

A = Window
B = Doorway
C = Doorway

PLAN OF HUT 13 AND
ATTACHED SHEEP FOLD

1st September 1983

TINKLER
CRAGS

9"

7"

5'5"

4'0"

17. Prynne's ink drawing of Hut 13 and attached sheepfold.

83

THE OVAL WINDOW

Annotated text

BEFORE *is* a relation, of degree two, but it is a relation for which not all the underlying domains are *simple*. AFTER is a semantically equivalent relation of degree three, with the property that all its domains *are* simple—in other words, AFTER is normalized.[1]

This condition says essentially that, given the present, the past and future are independent of each other.[2]

1. 'Mathematically speaking, BEFORE is a relation, of degree two, but it is a relation for which not all the underlying domains are *simple*. (A simple domain is one in which all elements are atomic.) AFTER is a semantically equivalent relation of degree three, with the property that all its domains are simple – in other words, AFTER is normalized. We choose to support only normalized relations in the relational approach because (a) as the example shows, this choice imposes no real restriction on what can be represented, and (b) the resulting simplification in data structure leads to corresponding simplifications in numerous other areas' (C. J. Date, *An Introduction to Database Systems*, 3rd edn., Reading, Massachusetts: Addison-Wesley Publishing Company, 1981, p. 87).

2. John G. Kemeny and J. Laurie Snell, *Finite Markov Chains* (Princeton: D. Van Nostrand Inc., 1960), p. 26. A Markov chain is a stochastic process with the property of 'memorylessness', whereby future outcomes can be predicted without reference to any circumstances preceding the point from which the prediction is made. As described by J. J. Martin, in a Markov chain 'the conditional probability of transitions to future states depends only on the state presently occupied by the system and not on the history of the system prior to entering that state' (*Bayesian Decision Problems and Markov Chains*, New York: Krieger Publishing Co., 1975, p. 5).

The shut inch lively as pin grafting
leads back to the gift shop, at a loss
for two-ply particles
                              set callow,
set bland and clean, wailing as when
to wait is block for scatter. Ah so,
the estrangement of the cause brings off
a surcease of the affect, even end-up
battered in sawdust. You cut your chin
on all this, like club members on the dot
by a winter blaze.
                        What can't be helped
is the vantage, private and inert; yet
in a twinkling[1] mind you, to pick up
elastic replacements on the bench code.

1. I Corinthians 15. 51-52: 'Behold, I shew you a mystery; We shall not all sleep, but we shall all be changed. / In a moment, in the twinkling of an eye, at the last trump: for the trumpet shall sound, and the dead shall be raised incorruptible, and we shall be changed'.

The phrase was used by the translator of *Wen fu*, the 'Essay on Literature', by Lu Chi (261-303), in a passage describing the poet's task and vision:

> Thus the poet will have mustered what for a hundred generations
>   awaited his pen,
> To be uttered in rimes for a thousand ages unheard.
> Let the full blown garden flowers of the ancients in their own
>   morning glory stand.
> To breathe life into late blossoms that have yet to bud will be his
>   sole endeavor.
> Eternity he sees in a twinkling,
> And the whole world he views in one glance.

(*Essay on Literature*, tr. Shih Hsiang Chen, Portland, Maine: Anthoesen Press, 1953, p. xxi). See pages 25 and 32.

Formerly in a proper tonic, the rain
would pelt and cure by the foam inlet.
    Smartly clad[1] they could only panic
      through the medium itself, **rabbit**[2] by proxy.
On both sides **smart guidance**[3] *ex* stock
makes for home like a cup cake over.
          Don't stare:
          Police aware:
it is a **defect coma,**[4] and it shows;
try it on, see if they'd want to care.

1. *The Times*, 22 August 1983, reporting a ZZ Top concert at Castle Donington's 'Monsters of Rock' festival: 'ZZ Top are a sight for sore eyes; they are smartly clad in pastels, absurd pink guitars and extravagantly styled beards, which is not to say that they are hell bent on pastiche; they are all excellent musicians with a total command of the blues based Texan boogie tradition.'

2. 'rabbit': London cab drivers' slang for gossip, the latest stories and rumours, etc.

3. 'smart guidance': referring generally to precision-guided weapons of all forms. In 1983 the most advanced systems were using laser or radar guidance (tested at RAF Spadeadam), while since 1991 these systems have largely been superseded by satellite guidance.

4. 'When the parabolic mirror's axis is inclined to the incident parallel rays, however, so that the union of reflected parallel rays does not lie on the $\mathbb{C}$ [i.e. the common optical centre line], then the reflected rays no longer unite with geometrical optics perfection. Rather, their union manifests the image defect called *coma* [...] the defect coma [...] is a result of improper deviations, produced by reflection or refraction, at different facets of the same ring zone' (J.D. Strong, *Concepts of Classical Optics*, San Francisco: W. H. Freeman and Co., 1958, p. 332).

Just a treat sod Heine you notice
the base going down, try to whistle
with a tooth broken. **Safe in our hands**[1]
won't cut up rough, at all, pent up
and boil over. **Fly my brother,**[2] he watches
at point of entry, only seeming to
have a heart for it. Thermal patchwork
will tell, sisal entreaty creams out.

1. *The Times*, 22 August 1983: 'Several local health authorities are now treating with scepticism the Prime Minister's statement during the election campaign that the service "is safe in our hands".' The then Prime Minister, Margaret Thatcher, had first used the phrase 'the National Health Service is safe with us' in her speech to the Conservative Party conference in October 1982, and repeated it, with variations, throughout the campaign preceding the general election in June 1983.

2 Shakespeare, *King Lear*, 2.i.29-33:

> I hear my father coming: pardon me:
> In cunning I must draw my sword upon you.
> Draw; seem to defend yourself; now quit you well.
> Yield: come before my father. Light, ho, here!
> Fly, brother. Torches, torches! So, farewell.

Coming through with your back turned
you'd never credit the trick aperture
in part-supply. **Being asked to cut
into the bone**[1] matches wishing to become
the one that asks and is sharply hurt.
To be controlled as a matter of urgency:[2]
don't turn, it's plasma leaking

          a tune on Monday

          a renewed drive[3]

          not doing enough

to reduce[4] the skin on a grape; the whole
falling short is wounded vantage in

          talk of the town.

1. *The Times*, 23 August 1983: 'The district administrator [of Bristol and Weston district health authority] [...] says that the fat has already been cut and now they are being asked to cut into the bone.'

2. 'Ministers believed that manpower in the health service needed to be controlled as a matter of urgency.' (ibid.)

3. 'There must be a renewed drive, with the help of all health service professions, to achieve economies and to reduce costs.' (ibid.)

4. 'Health authorities were told yesterday that they were not doing enough to reduce staff in the health service.' (ibid.)

Low in these windows you **let forth**
a **life**long transfusion, as **by the selfsame**
          hand that made these wounds.[1]
Keep back from the upper notch, running below
a steep flurry of pollen like a pestilence
        rated up for coverage.
The two main shadows over the future[2] tense
are pity and the lack of it, win or lose:
banking on form, the bright lozenge marks
rape swathing under a bandaged sleeve.
Stacking the calls as they come in to land
    a perdita d'occhio[3] the drill rigs
      make a ring of fire, welded on.

1. Shakespeare, *The Tragedy of Richard the Third*, 1.ii.5-13:

> Poor key cold figure of a holy king,
> Pale ashes of the house of Lancaster,
> Thou bloodless remnant of that royal blood,
> Be it lawful that I invoke thy ghost
> To hear the lamentations of poor Anne,
> Wife to thy Edward, to thy slaughtered son,
> Stabbed by the selfsame hand that made these wounds.
> Lo, in these windows that let forth thy life,
> I pour the helpless balm of my poor eyes.

2. *Financial Times*, 24 August 1983: 'The [National Institute of Economic and Social Research] identifies two main shadows over the future prospects for the world economy: the effect of large US budget deficits on interest rates, and the linked problems of many third world countries in servicing and repayment of their debts to Western banks.'

3. 'As far as the eye can see'; with the additional suggestion of something too large or sublime to be taken in.

Somewhere else in the **market** it's called
a **downward**[1] sell-out, to get there first
and cut open a fire break. Less won't do,
more isn't on either. How **a gang of boys
set her face alight with a flaming aerosol can,
"her mouth was sealed up by the burns."**[2]
Attention is **low in historic terms**[3] and will
drift down,[4] seeming to falter slowly and
making excuses for the money numbers[5] ahead.

1. *The Times*, 25 August 1983: 'Forecasts of a 7½ per cent inflation rate by the end of next year and gloomy prognoses for the economy by the National Institute for Economic and Social Research contributed to the stock market's downward spiral yesterday.'

2. *The Times*, 22 August 1983: 'A girl aged nine yesterday described how a gang of skinheads set her face alight with a flaming aerosol can. Victoria Mullarkey, of Tallaght, Dublin, could not open her eyes for two days after the attack last week. The girl's mother, Mrs Patricia Mullarkey, said: "She was not able to talk because her mouth was sealed up by the burns".'

3. *Financial Times*, 24 August 1983: 'Profits are expected to remain low, in historic terms.'

4. 'Improvement in export performance next year is predicted on the assumptions that sterling will drift lower.' (ibid.)

5. *Financial Times*, 25 August 1983: 'Last year, however, the Fed was frightened almost out of its wits by the impending foreign debt crisis; to save the banking system it adopted a new policy of forcing interest rates down, and making excuses for the money numbers.'

It is deep cold, high cloud on the grill
to hear the swish of a month overhead
in snow on the bush, bird in the hand.
The notice is not lit by cycle time,
blinded to limit the revenant by overt
loss of balance. **"He takes pity with him
and makes it possible for him to enter the sea"**[1]
with the reflex of **naked armour,**[2] unplayed
under the lintel.
              The vantage stops off
in arc-light at frosted glass, yet all is shaded
and clumsily mobile. Lately **poor eyes.**[3]

1. Max Walleser, 'The Life of Nagarjuna from Tibetan and Chinese Sources', *Asia Major*, Hirth anniversary volume, 1923, p. 447. The translation from the German, by the London bookseller and publisher Arthur Probsthain, is curiously literal, and the first part of the sentence would be more idiomatically rendered 'he takes pity on him'. Nagarjuna, the great Buddhist philosopher and teacher, was probably born in Southern India some time during the second century AD, but the sources drawn on by Walleser (1874-1954), one of the leading German Indologists of his time, were of much later date and heavily embellished with legend. The 'he' in this extract is a Bodhisattva (i.e. one who through compassion has attained one of the four sublime states), named Maha naga, who met Nagarjuna on his wanderings and led him 'to the Dragon Palace under the sea, where he received further instruction' (Alice Getty, *The Gods of Northern Buddhism*, Oxford: The Clarendon Press, 1928, p. 41).

2. Shakespeare, *The Rape of Lucrece*:

> Here pale with fear he doth premeditate
> The dangers of his loathsome enterprise,
> And in his inward mind he doth debate
> What following sorrow may on this arise:
> Then looking scornfully, he doth despise
> His naked armour of still slaughter'd lust,
> And justly thus controls his thoughts unjust:
> 'Fair torch, burn out thy light, and lend it not
> To darken her whose light excelleth thine.'
>   (*ll.* 183-191)

3. Shakespeare, *Richard III* (see notes to p. 96).

What if the outlook is likely to cut short
by an **inspired fear in the bond market.**[1]
The place itself is a birthday prank:

   current past the front,
   en première ligne

like stone dust on **strips of brighter green.**[2]
Given to allergic twitching, the frame
compounds for invertible counterpoint
and waits to see. **A view is a window**
on the real data, not a separate copy
of that data,[3] or a **lower surplus in oil**
and erratic items such as precious stones,
aircraft[4] and **the corpses of men, tigers**
fish and pythons, "all in a confused tangle."[5]
   Changes to the real data
are visible through the view; and operations
against the view are converted,[6] through
a kind of **unofficial window on Treasury policy,**[7]
into operations on the real data.
To this world given over, now safely,
work makes free[8] logic joined to the afterlife.

1. *Financial Times*, 25 August 1983: 'A very high deficit imposes high interest rates regardless of monetary policy, because it inspires fear in the bond markets'.

2. Sir Archibald Geikie, *Scottish Reminiscences* (Glasgow: James Maclehose and Sons, 1904), describing his visit to the island of Raasay, in 1855: 'Many of the cottages still retained their roofs, and in one of the deserted houses I found on a shelf a copy of the Bible [...] When I revisited the place a few days ago [i.e. in 1904], only ruined walls and strips of brighter herbage showed where the crofts had been' (p. 227; quoted in Eric Richards, *A History of the Highland Clearances*, London: Croom Helm, 1982, p. 484). Cf. '[W]e were passing [...] a heap of scattered stones round which was a belt of green grass – green, and as it seemed rich' – i.e. the remains of a hut where goats had been milked close to the door. *Journals of Dorothy Wordsworth*, ed. De Selincourt, vol. 1 (London, 1952), p. 372.

3. C.J. Date, *An Introduction to Database Systems*: 'A view is a "window" on the real data, not a separate copy of that data. Changes to the real data are visible through the view; and [...] operations against the view are converted into operations on the real data' (p. 162).

4. *The Times*, 25 August 1983: 'The poor July trade figures were affected by a lower surplus on oil trade and erratic items such as precious stones and aircraft'.

5. Newspaper not identified, probably 26 August 1983, reporting the centenary of the 1883 eruption of Krakatoa: 'The island of Krakatoa was blown completely off the map by the eruption. Only a couple of reefs remained, and a submarine cavity 1000ft deep. Other islands in the strait vanished and new ones appeared. The waters themselves seemed truly apocalyptic. Floating in a sea of pumice were the remnants of houses and trees, and the corpses of men, tigers, fish, and pythons, all in a confused tangle. One man avoided death in the swirling seas only by holding on to the back of an alligator, another by clinging to a drowning cow.'

6. Date, *An Introduction to Database Systems*, p. 162.

7. *Financial Times*, 25 August 1983: 'The National Institute of Economic and Social Research used to be known as the Treasury in Exile [...] its forecasting work, which was very like that of the official side, was useful both as a kind of unofficial window on Treasury policy, through which business could take its lead, and as a check on the Treasury's own work.'

8. *Arbeit macht Frei*, slogan set above the gateway to Auschwitz.

So they **burned their boats,** looking on
as the frontage **went up**[1] and footlights
blinked in the watercourse. From each
throat at its fan opening they spoke out
their force of numbers. **Either a point
object or its image point is said
to be real when the light propagates
through it**[2] by ash bluff to printed charcoal.
Count back the poll capture, fun running
like paint from blue to blue over
in the funnel head **(sad despair, &c).**[3]

1. *The Cambridge Evening News*, 1 September 1983: 'Two of Cambridge's oldest boat houses were destroyed in a spectacular £250,000 blaze last night [...] It was just after 11 pm when the historic boathouses, one owned by the '99 Rowing Club and the other by the CRA, went up in flames [...] Members of the boat clubs broke into the blazing buildings to rescue their boats, some worth over £2,000, flinging them into the river now illuminated by the flames. Teams of firemen, battling with the inferno, had to stop the distraught club members from making any more sallies on the boat houses as flaming pieces of debris came crashing onto the towpath.'

2. 'Either a point object or its image point is said to be real when the light propagates through it [...] An object point is said to be virtual when the light propagates toward it, but is refracted or reflected in front of it' (J.D. Strong, *Concepts of Classical Optics*, San Francisco: W. H. Freeman and Co., 1958, p. 254).

3. The refrain from the song 'Now O now I needs must part', commonly known as the Frog Galliard, by John Dowland, included in his 1597 *Book of Songs or Ayres*:

> Now O now I needs must part,
> parting though I absent mourne,
> absence can no ioye empart,
> ioye once fled can not returne.
> While I liue I needs must loue,
> loue liues not when hope is gone,
> now at last despayre doth proue,
> loue deuided loueth none:
> Sad dispaire doth driue me hence,
> this dispaire vnkindness sends.
> If that parting be offence,
> it is she which then offendes.

Sideways in the mirror and **too slow
to take up,**[1] it is the point of death. Not
lost from the track as passing its peak
but the cycle burns out on the axle,
quenching a thirst with lip salve slicked
on the ridge of its porridge bowl. Still
spoilt by bad temper the screen relives
a guessed anxiety: **wounds were his feast,
his life to life a prey.**[2]
                            The internal view
assumes an infinite linear address space,[3]
a table on which are laid out all
the rival manuals of self-sufficiency.
Spring up, O well; sing unto it:[4] but
the answer is **a pool of values**[5] in prime
hock to a pump and its **trade-offs.**[6]
That's putting it mildly, by repute.

1. *Financial Times*, 24 August 1983: 'The growth of output in the past two years has been too slow to take up much of the surplus capacity left by the recession'.

2. From Ovid's story of Erysichthon, who was consumed with hunger as punishment for violating the sacred grove of Ceres.

> His Muscles with a furious Bite he tore,
> Gorg'd his own tatter'd Flesh, and gulph'd his Gore.
> Wounds were his Feast, his Life to Life a Prey,
> Supporting Nature by its own decay.

Metamorphoses, VIII; translation by Thomas Vernon, in *Ovid's Metamorphoses, translated into English verse under the direction of Sir Samuel Garth, by Mr Dryden, Mr Addison, and other eminent hands* (London, 1717).

3. Date, *An Introduction to Database Systems*, p. 24: 'The internal view is a very low-level representation of the entire database [...] at one remove from the physical level, since it does not deal in terms of physical records or blocks [...] (Basically the internal view assumes an infinite linear address space. Details of how this address space is mapped to physical storage are highly implementation-specific and are not explicitly addressed in the architecture.)'

4. Numbers 21, 16-18: 'And from thence they went to Beer: that is the well wherof the Lord spake unto Moses, Gather the people together, and I will give them water. / Then Israel sang this song, Spring up, O well; sing ye unto it. / The princes digged the well, the nobles of the people digged it, by the direction of the lawgiver, with their staves.'

5. Date, *An Introduction to Database Systems*, p. 65: 'A domain is a pool of values from which the actual values appearing in a given column are drawn'.

6. *Financial Times*, 25 August 1983: 'The process enables us to study trade-offs – for example, between unemployment and inflation – in the only scientific way.'

Do be serious they say, all the time
in the world mounts a deficit
of choice moments fluffed and spilled.
Is misery worse than not knowing its cause,
the wrong fuel in a spirit lamp? The case
rests on tarmac already crumbled
in a pre-recorded dawn chorus:

**when the furniture was removed
he pulled out the window frames, threw down
the roof, and pushed in the walls.**[1] Yet short-
winded the pay-bed recycles a bad debt
as if nothing else counted, as if **there are
two distinct and mutually exclusive actions
depending on one test.**[2] *Viz*, oilseed
is a fashion laid out like data, the view
loops round from the test drill sponsor
like a bird on the wing. Think now
or pay now and think later, the **levels
of control nesting**[3] presume a reason
to cut back only and keep mum.

1. From a report in *The Inverness Courier*, describing the evictions of cottagers living on the Balfour estate at Strathconon, about 30 miles west of Inverness, at Whitsun 1850. Some of the cottagers had 'promised to leave by Lammas', while others were removed at Whitsun itself:

> The officer again proceeded to the house of Mrs. Campbell. No promise could be got from the woman to remove at any time. I saw the sad glance the poor daughter cast to the green hill before her as she said the words – it revealed the deep sorrow of her heart to leave the scene for ever; but I felt, whilst sympathising with her, that the Allwise Creator had permitted few of his rational creatures to indulge feelings of this nature in profitless idleness. No promise to remove could be obtained, and, assisted by the women, the furniture was removed. Whilst this labour was proceeding, one of the sons appeared from a neighbouring house and lent a hand. When the furniture was removed, he pulled out the window frames, threw down the roof, and pushed in the walls. So little animosity did he seem to feel, that he was most anxious to 'treat' the officers to a 'dram'.

> Quoted in Eric Richards, *A History of the Highland Clearances*, London: Croom Helm, 1982, p. 398.

2. 'The ELSE is a red herring, serving no purpose here. It should be used only when there are two distinct and mutually exclusive actions depending on one test.' Brian W. Kernighan and P. J. Plauger, *The Elements of Programming Style*, New York: McGraw-Hill, 1974, p. 32.

3. 'Declarations are neatly aligned, and the executable statements are staggered so as to indicate several levels of control nesting.' Kernighan and Plauger, *The Elements of Programming Style*, p. 23.

So what you do is enslaved non-stop
to perdition of sense by leakage
                into the cycle: one man's meat
better late than never. Motor life says
the branch office, a picture is not a window.
In a recursive procedure, the method
of solution is defined in terms of itself;[1] as,
within the chain-guard, cold is the meaning
of heat notably absent. The arctic tern
stays put wakefully, each following suit
by check according to rote; it's precious little,
only smoke damage where that came from.

1. 'A powerful tool for reducing apparent complexity is recursion. In a recursive procedure, the method of solution is defined in terms of itself. That is, each part of the routine handles only a small piece of the strategy, then calls the other parts of the routine as needed to handle the rest.' Kernighan and Plauger, *The Elements of Programming Style*, p. 73.

As what next if you can't, **silent fire**[1]
dumped in a skip and sun boiling over
the sack race. Best before too late, with
loath to depart[2] in the buff envelope torn across.
I'm finger-perfect by the yard, not like
the ancient sponges putting in question
another glad hand from the puppet dictator.
From the skip there is honey and bent metal,
romantic on trade plates: **PUT SKIP EDIT,**
PUT SKIP DATA,[3] **the control flow structure**[4]
demands a check that subscripts do not exceed
array dimensions.[5] That is the regimen,
the bin liner of the second subject, holding
our tongues like brevet clients on call.

1. Wordsworth, *The Excursion,* IV. 1071-74:

> Like power abides
> In man's celestial spirit; virtue thus
> Sets forth and magnifies herself, thus feeds
> A calm, a beautiful, and silent fire,
> From the encumbrances of mortal life.

2. A 'loath to depart' in Elizabethan times was a piece of music played as a farewell, either at the end of a performance or for the departure of friends. Composers such as John Dowland (1563-1626) and Giles Farnaby (1563-1640) wrote pieces with this title.

3. **PUT SKIP EDIT** and **PUT SKIP DATA** are computer programming instructions in Fortran and PL/I (Programming Language One); see Kernighan and Plauger, *The Elements of Programming Style*, pp. 24, 33.

4. 'As much as possible, a program should be written so the control flow structures lead the reader quickly and directly to an understanding of what the program does.' (*The Elements of Programming Style*, p. 35)

5. 'Does the program read a parameter to define an array size? Then test that it does not exceed the array bounds [...] Some compilers [...] allow a check during execution that subscripts do not exceed array dimensions' (*The Elements of Programming Style*, p. 85).

Within the frame the match-play is staggered,
to protect the list from its first mistake.
Skip and slip are the antinomian free gifts
mounted on angle-iron reflexes, as sick pay
predates a check to recovery. You're flat out?
But the method sorts **downward**,[1] wired up
from the NCR cashpoint; you must choose the order
of choice, on the nail from which shadows hang.
What else **null else**[2] just else if before
out into the garden with **overshoot**,[3] the
moon is bright as snowy day. In broad
strip neon it ranks as a perfect crime.

1. *The Times*, 25 August 1983: 'Forecasts of a 7½ per cent inflation rate by the end of next year and gloomy prognoses for the economy by the National Institute for Economic and Social Research contributed to the stock market's downward spiral yesterday.'

2. 'A null ELSE [i.e. an ELSE instruction with no following statement] indicates that the programmer knows that trouble lies ahead and is trying to defend against it.' (Kernighan and Plauger, *The Elements of Programming Style*, p. 47)

3. *Financial Times*, 24 August 1983: 'The immediate concern in the U.S. is what will happen to monetary policy if the money supply continues to over-shoot its targets.'

In the margin tinted love breaks off
to spot bravura by scrub wintergreen.
Ill met[1] on this road, by invitation
they do keep up while in keeping and
sly good humour. Or sit and choke or
die too, you must mind only so much,
looping ahead with do and while[2] and
calling softly like a fish. **Test and store**[3]
alla buona, **failing to respond,**[4] a
sweet smile intent with the marker
in **default values;**[5] slowness of gaze
goes down with you, flickering to meet
in both the turn for good.

1. Shakespeare, *A Midsummer Night's Dream*, II.i.60: 'Ill met by moonlight, proud Titania.'

2. 'The control structures of a language provide the framework of a program. These include decision making with IF and ELSE, looping with DO and WHILE; statement grouping; and procedures or subroutines and functions' (Kernighan and Plauger, *The Elements of Programming Style*, p. 31).

3. 'If we do not fret over making a few "unnecessary" tests, we can unsnarl the tangle of branches with a general "test and store" subroutine, which decides whether one specified direction represents a legal move, and saves it.' (*The Elements of Programming Style*, p. 61)

4. *Financial Times*, 25 August 1983: 'Britain's export performance is failing to respond to the improving climate of world trade and the better competitiveness of UK manufacturers, according to official figures out yesterday.'

5. 'If input parameters are supplied by name, you can use default values in a graceful way. If some parameter is normally given a certain value, build that value into the program; then if users do not specify its value, they will get the built in value "by default".' (*The Elements of Programming Style*, p. 94)

Droplock[1] to gab

       off you steel

   by wed foot

       and fall under

fur on the gate

       Tivoli Tivoli

and if flatter so

       the better to win

O spite reserve

       my mitten's

   bred sodden

       at all given to

pad out, fill in

       hold this piece

forth with and

       so on go on

to the lammas

       of forbidden let

      red

       ground

1. *The Times*, 22 August 1981: 'The novelty this week is a Droplock stock [...] The basic idea is that the stock starts life with a coupon tied to short term money market rates. So, if interest rates rise in the early years, the income paid to the investor also rises [...] Should interest rates fall below a predetermined level (announced at the time of the original issue), then the coupon on the stock "locks" and remains fixed for the remainder of the stock's life.'

At the onset of the single life
it is joined commonly to what
                          is untasted, lettered out
along the oval window's rim.

And casting the eave forward, in
the first delivery you do know
                          this talc in breath,
marking the **helm wind**[1] as it cools.

It fans the rim on the inside
of the purlin itself, the tenon gives back
                          exactly your life task
and for the trained level. Grind up

to the hatchment there, they are later
as to the perfect clank. No time
                          first-round, first leg, with
dearer love he too could only panic

through the medium. Hold your chin
to the relief coach; I am a woodland fellow
                          sirloin parted formerly
that always loved a great fire.[2]

The window glints now in the lee wave,
fed with light up-ended. **Crape put out
                          on the hives.**[3] Life cover
streams under, **the master I speak of**

**ever keeps a good fire. Give a low
whistle,**[4] such country cannot be burnt;
                          fit the rebate, **but
sure, he is the prince of the world.**

We will cast on the half then and find out
the neural crest below, an inquest
                          wrought with frost without
snow-marking on the run to try

1. 'Wind tends to descend hill slopes more forcibly if an inversion layer is present above the summit [...] The best example of this process in Britain is provided by the 'helm wind' of Crossfell and the neighbouring Pennine slopes in Cumberland and Westmorland. On days when the north-east wind prevails [...] a characteristic wall of cloud is seen lying along, or just above, the summits of the Pennines [...] Parallel to this cloud, known as the 'helm' – a word probably (though not quite certainly) expressive of the helmet like nature of the cloud – there lies, at the same level but four or five miles distant to the south west, another line of clouds sometimes continuous, sometimes broken up into fragments' (Gordon Manley, *Climate and the British Scene*, London: Collins, 1952, p. 148).

2. Shakespeare, *All's Well that Ends Well*, IV.v.50-59 (Lavatch, the Clown, speaking): 'I am a woodland fellow, sir, that always loved a great fire; and the master I speak of, ever keeps a good fire. But, sure, he is the prince of the world; let his nobility remain in's court. I am for the house with the narrow gate, which I take to be too little for pomp to enter: some that humble themselves may; but the many will be too chill and tender, and they'll be for the flow'ry way that leads to the broad gate and the great fire'.

3. Putting bees into mourning along with the rest of a family was a widespread rural custom persisting well into the twentieth century. For an early account, see Anne Pratt, *Dawnings of Genius: or, The Early Lives of Some Eminent Persons of the Last Century*, London: Charles Knight and Co., 1841: 'Many traditionary practices prevail in Cornwall among the cottagers. It was usual, even very lately, to put a piece of black crape on the bee-hives when the master of a house died; and, if this was omitted, it was fancied that the bees would fly from the spot' (p. 12). Thomas Hardy mentioned a Dorset version of this tradition in his 1884 story 'Interlopers at the Knap': 'It was the universal custom thereabout to wake the bees by tapping at their hives whenever a death occurred in the household, under the belief that if this were not done the bees themselves would pine away and perish during the ensuing year' (*Wessex Tales*, London: Macmillan and Co., 1888, Vol II, p. 46).

4. 'By now my mental state had become something similar to that experienced by lone yachtsmen: a curious blend of the very practical and the quite fantastic [...] Somewhere in the Lepontine Alps I became very interested in the activities of marmots [...] Each colony protects itself with a ring of look outs, and the commonest sound in some valleys is the piercing wolf whistle that these sentries give out as a warning [...] Sometimes they were the only company I had, and so I had begun talking to them, in a harmless fashion. I would give a sharp whistle in passable imitation, and shout out "Hi".' David Brett, *High Level: The Alps from End to End*, London: Victor Gollancz, 1983, pp. 83-4.

the spoil and waste in a white suit.
Speak truly along the lip there, **let**
           his nobility remain in's
court. I am for the house again

and the egg-timer, give the sweet air
back as nipped by the bud of ruin:
           three to one herring.[5]
Arms in sisal **with the narrow gate**

over-arched, knocking at the septum,
which I take to be too little for pomp
           to enter a pleasant fee,
their faces are part-eaten. This is the place

where, deaf to meaning, the life stands
out in extra blue. **Some that humble**
           themselves at the songbook
may turn the page enchanted; **but**

the many will be too chill below
in profile, **and tender**-limbed
           in the foil wrap.
They'll be for the flow'ry way and draw

a sharp breath by flutter action, do it
quickly, tongue tied. **That leads**
           to the broad gate
and the great fire, and deaf to the face

soundlessly matched to the summit.
We go over. The dip stands down
           in the oval window, in
the blackened gutter stop of the newly born.

5. 'Some People say, ah, but things were much cheaper in them days, quite correkt, but they were Just as dear in proportion as now, in fact more so. Scors of famleys were brought up on potatos, turnips, and Bread, with what was called Pork lard and Treackle, with a change of herring. Were they a big famley often as not they would have to go three of them to one herring'(*I Walked By Night; being the Life & History of the King of the Norfolk Poachers, written by Himself*, 1st edn 1935; Waveney: Boydell Press, 1975, p. 88).

As they parted, she heard his horse cry out,[1]
by the rustic lodge in a flurry of snow.
A child's joy, a toy with a snowstorm,
flakes settling in white prisms, to slide
to a stop. The flask is without frame,
metaldehyde safe in cold store. **There
is a snow-down on that sand hillock,
the stars are snowing, do you see it there:[2]
bright moonlight whitens the pear blossom.[3]**
You listen out by the oval window, as
calm waves flow onward to the horizon.[4]

1. From no. 6 of 'Fourteen Lyrics' by Wen T'ing-yün (812-870), translated by Lois Fusek and included in her edition of *Among the Flowers* (New York: Columbia University Press, 1982). The volume is a complete translation of the collection of the same title of five hundred Chinese lyrics compiled by Chao Ch'ung-tso at the time of the Later Shu dynasty (mid-10th century AD).

> In the jade tower bright with moonlight, she remembers.
> The willow branches were long and graceful that spring.
> Outside the gate the grass grew luxuriantly.
> As they parted, she heard his horse cry out.
> (p. 38)

2. Wyndham Lewis, *The Enemy of the Stars* (London: Desmond Harmsworth, 1932), Arghol speaking: 'Are those great stars wonder portions of an absolute, magnitude of magnitudes, or no more than the electric bulbs in the workshop? We are beneath the coverlet of earth, as to the roots of our essence. Esse is percipi, at least we see – that is all that can be said for us. Our eyes are on a par with the stellar universes. Our brains are sick with the distances achieved by our instruments. – There is a snow down on that sand hillock, the stars are snowing, do you see it there?' (p. 31)

3. From no. 9 of the 'Fourteen Lyrics' by Wen T'ing-yün, in *Among the Flowers*, as above:

> Bright moonlight in the house whitens the pear blossom.
> Unending miles of mountains and passes keep them apart.
> A pair of golden geese soar through the sky.
> Traces of tears dampen her embroidered robe.
> (p. 39)

4. From no. 4 of 'Five Lyrics' by Sun Kuang hsien (898-968), in *Among the Flowers*, as above:

> The morning rain bathes the blue grotto on the dark cliff.
> Over the flowers they call each other to the south stream.
> They set sail in a skiff of magnolia wood.
> The calm waves flow onward to the horizon.
> (p. 148)

Her wrists shine white like the frosted snow;[1]
they call each other to the south stream.[2]
The oval window is closed in life,
by the foot-piece of the stapes.[3] Chill shadows
fall from the topmost eaves,[4] clear waters
run beside the blossoming peach.[5] Inside
this window is the perilymph of the vestibule.[3]
    Now O now I needs must part,
    parting though I absent mourne.[6]
It is a child's toy, shaken back in
myopic eddies by the slanting bridge:[7]
toxic; dangerous fire risk, bright moonlight
floods the steps like a cascade of water.[4]

1. From 'Five Lyrics' by Wei Chuang (836-910):

> The girl pouring wine is as fair as the moon.
> Her wrists shine white like the frosted snow.
> Do not return home before you have grown old,
> To return home is surely to break your heart!
> (*Among the Flowers*, 60)

2. From 'Five Lyrics' by Sun Kuang-hsien (898-968):

> The morning rain bathes the blue grotto on the dark cliff.
> Over the flowers they call each other to the south stream.
> (*Among the Flowers*, 148)

3. 'Behind and above the promontory is an oval window, the *fenestra vestibule*, closed in life by the foot piece of the stapes. Inside this window is the perilymph of the vestibule.' (R. J. Last, *Anatomy: Regional and Applied*, Edinburgh, London and New York: Churchill Livingstone, 1978, p. 449)

4. From 'Five Lyrics' by Sun Kuang-hsien:

> Bright moonlight floods the steps like a cascade of water.
> The golden knocker clatters when the door is being closed.
> Chill shadows fall from the topmost eaves.
> The curtain is trailing loose on its hook.
> (*Among the Flowers*, 147)

5. From 'Five Lyrics' by Wei Chuang:

> Clear waters run beside the blossoming peach.
> Mandarin ducks dip themselves in a cool flow.
> (*Among the Flowers*, 61)

6. Dowland, 'The Frog Galliard', as p. 105 above.

7. From 'Five Lyrics' by Wei Chuang:

> I can still remember how happy I was south of the river.
> Then I was young, and my spring robes were a light silk.
> I would ride my horse by the slanting bridge.
> (*Among the Flowers*, 60)

Snow-blinded, we hold our breath;
the echo trembles like a pinpoint, on
each line of the hooded screen. It is life
at the rim of itself, in face of the brow
closed to sorrow. **A pale white light
from the east is shining in the window,**[1]
a flowering spray in the glow of the mirror.[2]
The internal view burns at this frame,
eyes frozen by calm. For full paralysis
of accommodation, three or four drops
should be instilled every fifteen minutes
for one or two hours. For the rest of
your life. **Sight wherein my joys do lie**[3]
on a pillow[4] white with shade, **brushed
in azure along the folding screen;**[5]
all day long, the red door is closed.[6]

1. From 'Five Lyrics' by Sun Kuang-hsien:

> The wings of the cock beat a hurried tattoo atop the wall.
> A pale white light from the east is shining in the window.
> Beyond the gate, the dawn orioles chatter.
> Behind the tower, the setting moon gleams.
>
> (*Among the Flowers*, 147)

2. From 'Fourteen Lyrics' by Wen T'ing yün:

> In the painted hall, all news is broken off.
> South of the river, grasses cover the banks.
> A flowering spray in the glow of the mirror.
> Who can know what her feelings are just now?
>
> (*Among the Flowers*, 39)

3. Dowland, 'The Frog Galliard', as above, p. 105.

4. From 'A Southern Song', seven lyrics by Wen T'ing yün:

> A gold curtain shimmers above her face.
> A patch of azure glows on her forehead.
> She rests on a pillow, beneath a quilt.
> Beyond the window screen, orioles sing,
> Making her miss him more.
>
> (*Among the Flowers*, 48)

5. From 'Seven Lyrics' by Niu Chiao (850?-920?):

> Wu Mountain is brushed in azure along the folding screen.
> The goddess of Ch'u still desires to be a floating cloud.
> Day and night, so many feelings fill her heart,
> But he has taken advantage of her love for him.
>
> (*Among the Flowers*, 87)

6. From 'Three Lyrics' by Mao Hsi chen (*circa*. AD 940):

> The pale blue of the sky harmonizes with the spring scene.
> Not a word has arrived from that pleasure seeking gallant.
> All the day long, the red door is closed.
> Parting's grief quietly breaks her heart.
>
> (*Among the Flowers*, 184)

So: from now on too, or soon lost,
the voice you hear is your own
revoked, on a **relative cyclical downturn**[1]
imaged in latent narrow-angle glaucoma.
Yet the snow picks up and infolds,
a mist of gold leaf lightly shimmers[2]
as **floating clouds go back to the mountains.**[3]
It is not quite a cabin, but **(in local speech)**
a *shield*,[4] in the elbow of upland water,
the sod roof almost gone but just under
its scar a rough opening: it is, in first
sight, the oval window. Last light foams
at this crest. The air lock goes cold
    in hot sun, blue streak under
lines swarming there, dung on all fours.
The **blur spot**[5] on both sides gives out
a low, intense hum, sharp-folded as
if to a feral rafter;
                the field is determined
by the *exit window*, the lens rim or stop
which, imaged into image space, subtends
the smallest angle at the centre.[6]
                         So small
here that the pin is bonelike and watched
with the backflood at steep echo,
in brown water clamped at vantage.
Mountains reach across the folds of the screen;[7]
green sedges line the path below cold mist
yet the stone step is boiling fast.
          Upon that dropping floor
          when hope is gone, the sky
          spoken like a roc's egg
in **cascaded magnification,**[8] runs in
and out and over: honey in snow.

1. *The Times*, 25 August 1983: 'This is not to say that there may not be some relative cyclical downturn next year or in 1985, but it would be cruel to hard won business confidence to confuse such, possibly minor, short term cycles with the longer process of recovery.'

2. From 'Two Lyrics' by Wei Ch'eng-pan (*c.* AD 910):

> A mist of gold leaf lightly shimmers on her silken gown.
> For a splendid gathering, she sings in the autumn night.
>
> (*Among the Flowers*, 162)

3. From 'Three Lyrics' by Mao Hsi-chen (c. AD 940):

> The lamp flickers behind her tiny window.
> The noisy swallows break her gloomy mood.
> The screen is closed, the fragrance gone.
> Floating clouds go back to the mountains.
>
> (*Among the Flowers*, 184)

4. '[Shelter] was provided in cottages called, to modernise the spelling, shielings or shiels. In local dialect and place names the name is usually shield or, in the more westerly areas of Cumberland and Westmorland, scale, latinised in documents as *scaling*.' (H.G. Ramm et. al., *Shielings and Bastles*, London: HMSO, 1970, p. 1).

5. 'If, for a cone of rays coming from S there is a corresponding cone of rays passing through P [...] the energy in the cone [...] reaches P, which is then referred to as a *perfect image* of S. The wave could conceivably arrive to form a finite patch of light, or *blur spot*, about P; it would still be an image of S but no longer a perfect one.' (Eugene Hecht and Alfred Zajac, *Optics*, 2nd ed., Reading, Massachusetts: Addison-Wesley Publishing Co., 1990, p. 128).

6. 'The field is determined by the *exit window* [...] The exit window is the lens rim or stop which, imaged into image space, subtends the smallest angle at the center of the exit pupil.' (Strong, *Concepts of Classical Optics*, p. 345).

7. From 'Seven Lyrics' by Niu Chiao (850?-920?):

> Gilded birds fly in the shining dark hair at her temples.
> She frowns with grief at the thinness of the spring mist.
> Her fragrant door is hidden by hibiscus blooms.
> Mountains reach across the folds of the screen.
>
> (*Among the Flowers*, 88)

8. 'The equations for magnification of a thick or thin lens, or of a system of surfaces, are obtained by cascading expressions for m that are appropriate to each component surface. First, we consider a thick lens for which the aggregate or cascaded magnification is m = m1m2.' (Strong, *Concepts of Classical Optics*, p. 330).

The clouds are white in a pale autumn sky.
Looking at the misty paths[1] I see this stooping
figure seeming to falter, in a thick compound
of adjustments,[2] sublimed in white flakes. Then
it clears down, she turns or round her
the sweet breath goes about, at midnight
murmuring. Extremities flexed and cold.
A light wind crosses the fragrant waters;[3]
deaf to reason I cup my hands, to
dew-drenched apricot flowers[4] and their
livid tranquillity. It has the merit
of being seen to hurt,[5] in her dream,
and then much further on, it does.

1. From 'One Lyric' by Yin O (*circa*. AD 920):

> The clouds at the border are white in a pale autumn sky.
> She sits alone by the window looking at the misty paths.
> The watch horn is sounding in the tower.
> Just at twilight, he returns very drunk.
>
> (*Among the Flowers*, 173-74)

2. *The Times*, 30 August 1983: 'The level of social security payments to the poor and unemployed cannot be considered a "principle" in and of itself. How could that be when any amount currently paid is a thick compound of adjustments for inflation over the years plus some real growth which only with difficulty can be linked to the objective measurements of subsistence made in the first days of National Assistance in the 1940s?'

3. From 'Three Lyrics' by Mao Hsi chen:

> She rolls a silken screen high, and gazes across the pond.
> Raindrops splash from the lotus just like tumbling pearls.
> It is late summer, the nights grow chill.
> A light wind crosses the fragrant waters.
>
> (*Among the Flowers*, 184)

4. From 'Fourteen Lyrics' by Wen T'ing yün:

> The dew drenched apricot flowers are sweet snowy balls.
> On the willow lined path there have been many partings.
> In the waning moonlight, the lamp is bright.
> She wakens to the sound of the dawn orioles.
>
> (*Among the Flowers*, 38)

5. *The Times*, 30 August 1983: 'The DHSS is said to be studying a reduction in the benefits paid to young people both by adjusting the basic rate [...] and cutting the rental allowances payable both to 18 year olds living at home and to all claimants living away from home [...] This, from Whitehall's point of view, has the merit of being seen to hurt (the Treasury is never convinced unless there are screams) but also, more important for the long run, to establish the violability of basic social benefits and do it for a group over which the political screams will not be too loud'.

Drawn to the window and beyond it,
by the heartfelt screen of a machine
tenderly lit sideways, the wish **to enter
the sea**[1] itself leaves snow dark as sand.
Pear blossoms drift through this garden,[2]
across the watcher's vantage clouded
by smoke from inside the **hut.**[3] Tunnel
vision as **she watches for his return,**[4]
face and flower shining each upon the other.[5]
    **So these did turn, return, advance,
    drawn back by doubt, put on by love.**[6]
Sort and merge,[7] there is burning along
this frame; and now before you see
you must, we need its name.

1. Walleser, The Life of Nagarjuna: see notes to p. 100.

2. From 'Three Lyrics' by Mao Hsi-chen:

> Pear blossoms drift through the garden like fragrant snow.
> High in the tower on a quiet night, wind strums the cheng.
>
> (*Among the Flowers*, 183)

3. 'One hut [no. 13 on the King Water site], though lying apart from the rest and latterly in use as a watcher's hut attached to a fold, belongs to the same tradition of building and illustrates the kind of turf roof, here of single pitch, which the shielings had' (Ramm et al., *Shielings and Bastles*, p. 14). In this case, however, the turf roof was probably a Victorian repair of the original.

4. From 'Seven Lyrics' by Niu Chiao:

> From the tower she watches for his return home.
> The window is chill as a drizzling rain clears.
>
> (*Among the Flowers*, 87).

5. From 'Fourteen Lyrics' by Wen T'ing yün:

> Mirrors, front and behind, reflect a flower,
> Face and flower shining each upon the other.
> Stitched in the silk of her bright new coat,
> Golden threaded partridges fly pair by pair.
>
> (*Among the Flowers*, 37)

6. Ben Jonson, *Love Restored* (1616), *ll*. 280-83:

> Haue men beheld the Graces daunce,
> Or seene the vpper Orbes to moue?
> So these did turne, returne, aduance,
> Drawne backe by doubt, put on by loue.
>
> (*The Works of Ben Jonson*, eds. Herford and Simpson, vol. VII;
> Oxford: The Clarendon Press, 1941, p. 385).

7. 'If the mouse comes out where it went in, this is not a path, so the program goes back to the appropriate RUNxx loop to continue searching the border where it left off. Otherwise it falls through to the SORT and MERGE loops, which determine the path to be printed out' (Kernighan and Plauger, *The Elements of Programming Style*, p. 70).

It is a CNS depressant. **Endless sorrow
rises from the misty waves,**[1] like a wick
in the light of conscience. Not feudal
nor slave-owning but the asiatic mode
as locally communal within a despotic state:
the slant of *imperium* coming sideways
**"through the competitive examination (*chin
shih*) on Confucian literature."**[2] Either contract
or fancy, each framing the other, **closed
in life.**[3] **A flickering lamp burns dimly
at the window,**[4] ready for snuff brilliance
which lights the mirror and shades the door.

1. From 'Five Lyrics' by Sun Kuang-hsien:

> The boat speeds along in the gusting wind.
> Her sleeves coral, she stands by the mast.
> She keeps turning back to the distant bay.
> Endless sorrow rises from the misty waves.

(*Among the Flowers*, 148)

2. 'The door to higher position and to the acquisition of wealth with which land could be bought was open to the person who had successfully passed through the competitive examination on Confucian literature' (Stephen Dunn, *The Fall and Rise of the Asiatic Mode of Production*, London: Routledge and Kegan Paul, 1982, p. 113, quoting I. V. Kachanovskii, *Slaveholding, Feudalism, or the Asiatic Mode of Production?*, Moscow, 1971). The term *chin-shih*, which does not occur in the Kachanovskii source, refers to the imperial examination as established during the Tang dynasty (around 730 AD). Candidates had to learn Confucian texts by heart and fill in blanks on the exam paper; those who were successful (the pass rate was on average 2%) were known as *Shen-shih*. The poem's preceding lines, beginning 'Not feudal / nor slave owning', roughly summarise Dunn's commentary on an unresolved debate among Marxist historians as to the nature of ancient Chinese society and the extent to which it could be accounted for in Marxist terms.

3. 'Behind and above the promontory is an oval window, the *fenestra vestibule*, closed in life by the foot piece of the stapes' (Last, *Anatomy*, p. 449).

4. From 'Fourteen Lyrics' by Wen T'ing yün:

> Because she thinks of him, she cannot sleep.
> A flickering lamp burns dimly at the window.

(*Among the Flowers*, 39)

Now the willows on the river are hazy like mist[1]
and the end is hazy like the meaning
which bridges its frozen banks. In the field
of view[2] a prismatic blur adds on
rainbow skirts to the outer leaves.

    They appropriated not the primary
conditions of labour but their results;[3]

    the waters of spring cross under
the bridge,[4] willow branches dip.[5]

    The denial of feudalism in China
always leads to political errors, of an
essentially Trotskyist order:[6]

    Calm is all nature as a resting wheel.[7]
The red candle flame shakes.[8]

1. From 'Fourteen Lyrics' by Wen T'ing yün:

> The willows on the river are hazy like mist.
> Wild geese fly in the sky as the moon fades.
>
> (*Among the Flowers*, 37)

2. 'The element limiting the size or angular breadth of the object that can be imaged by the system is called the field stop or F.S. – it determines the field of view of the instrument' (Hecht and Zizac, *Optics*, p. 149).

3. 'In the ancient East [...] "the ruling strata and groups [...] usurped primarily not the means of production as such but their management; they appropriated not the primary conditions of labor but their results".' (Dunn, pp. 106-07, quoting Ostrovitianov and Sterbalova in *Novyi mir*, no. 12, 1972).

4. From 'Fourteen Lyrics' by Wen T'ing yün:

> The waters of spring cross under the bridge.
> By the railing, her heart is about to break.
>
> (*Among the Flowers*, 40)

5. From 'Fourteen Lyrics' by Wen T'ing yün:

> In the painted hall, long she waits for him.
> Beyond the balcony, willow branches dip low.
>
> (*Among the Flowers*, 39)

6. 'Lominadze [...] maintained that the type of relations existing in the Chinese countryside could be called feudalism only in a very conditional way [...] Lominadze wished to call these relationships the Asiatic mode of production, as Marx had, but Godes protests [...] The precise words used by Godes at this point deserve close attention: "It turns out that the denial of feudalism in China, or the theory of it, always leads to political errors, and errors of an essentially Trotskyist order".' (Dunn, pp. 31-32).

7. Wordsworth, 'Sonnet: Written in very Early Youth':

> Calm is all nature as a resting wheel.
> The Kine are couch'd upon the dewy grass;
> The Horse alone, seen dimly as I pass,
> Is cropping audibly his later meal.

8. From 'Five Lyrics' by Sun Kuang hsien:

> A smoky mist of azure softly curls around.
> The red candle flame shakes with laughter.
>
> (*Among the Flowers*, 147)

In **darkness by day**[1] we must press on,
giddy at the tilt of **a negative crystal.**[2]
The toy is childish, almost below speech
lip-read by swaying lamps. **It is not
so hard to know as it is to do:**[3]
wresting the screen before the eyelet lost
to speech tune you blame the victim.
Pity me! **These petals, crimson and pink,**[4]
are cheque stubs, spilling chalk in **a mist
of soft azure.**[5] At the last we want
unit costs plus VAT, patient grading:
made to order, made to care, poised
at the nub of avid sugar soap.

1. From 'The Nine Songs', Song IX, 'The Mountain Spirit (Shan-kuei)':

> High on the top of the hill I stand all alone;
> Below me the clouds sweep past in droves.
> All is murk and gloom. Ch'iang! Darkness by day!
> The east wind blows gust on gust, spreading magic rain.
>
> (Arthur Waley, *The Nine Songs: A Study of Shamanism in Ancient China*, London: George Allen and Unwin Ltd., 1955, p. 53)

2. 'Compression partially orients otherwise randomly oriented anisotropic oscillators. The birefringence thus induced is that of a negative crystal with the optical axis parallel to the direction of compression.' (Strong, *Concepts of Classical Optics*, p. 154).

3. 'The ways of employing words and forming expressions are indeed infinitely varied. But, accordingly, the various degrees of beauty and excellence achieved needs must bear criticism. When I compose my own works, I am more keenly aware of the ordeal. Constantly present is the feeling of regret that the meaning apprehended does not represent the objects observed; and, furthermore, words fail to convey the meaning. The fact is, it is not so hard to know as it is to do.' (Li Chi, *Wen fu (Essay on Literature)*, tr. Shih-Hsiang Chen, Portland, Maine: Anthoesen Press, 1953, p. xix).

4. From 'Three Lyrics' by Li Hsün (855-930):

> Two swallows fly in the misty rain outside the curtains.
> Petals fall over the steps in piles of crimson and pink.
> She strums a melody on the precious zither.
> Her heart goes after that boat so far away.
>
> (*Among the Flowers*, 193)

5. From 'Five Lyrics' by Sun Kuang hsien (898-968):

> A smoky mist of azure softly curls around.
> The red candle flame shakes with laughter.
>
> (*Among the Flowers*, 147)

Standing by the window I heard it,
while waiting for the turn. In hot light
and chill air it was the crossing flow
of even life, hurt in the mouth but
exhausted with passion and joy. Free
to leave at either side, at the fold line
found in threats like herbage, the watch
is fearful and promised before. The years
jostle and burn up as a trust plasma.
Beyond help it is joy at death itself:
a toy hard to bear, laughing all night.

To the Lammas

It is not quite a cabin, but (in local speech)
a *shield*, in the elbow of upland water,
the sod roof almost gone but just under
its scar a rough opening: it is, in first
sight, the oval window. Last light foams
at this crest. The air lock goes cold
     in hot sun, blue streak under
lines swarming there, dung on all fours.
The blur spot on both sides gives out
a low, intense hum, sharp-folded as
if to a feral rafter

On the cover of the original edition of *The Oval Window* there is a photograph showing a window-like opening in the wall of a ruined 'shield', or shieling, a a rough stone hut built by medieval farmers to house themselves and their families during the summer transhumance. This particular hut is one of a number of similar buildings at Tinkler Crags, on Askerton North Moor, a desolate area near the village of Gilsland, in Cumbria, not far from Hadrian's Wall. Those farming communities, with their livestock and some basic provisions, would have travelled, each May, some fifteen or twenty miles from the district around Carlisle and the Solway Firth, following river valleys upwards to these open pastures about 800 feet above sea level, the valley in this case being that of a stream called the King Water, which flows southwestwards to join the River Irthing near the small town of Brampton. The huts at Tinkler Crags were built alongside meanders of the stream to allow ready access to fresh water. This stretch of moor, or 'shielding ground', would be occupied until early August – traditionally until Lammas Day, August 1st – at which point the families would retrace their steps to the lowland settlement. The practice of transhumance in this part of northern England died out around the end of the seventeenth century, but later generations of local farmers adapted some of the abandoned buildings for their own needs, including the remains of the hut in question, which in Victorian times had a sheepfold constructed next to it. The opening in the wall was not, strictly speaking, a 'window', more of a smoke vent (although for the most part smoke from the interior would have escaped through the doorway), and the 'sod roof', turves laid over spars cut from whatever wood was to hand, 'feral rafters', has now completely 'gone' (although a photograph from 1970 showed it still fairly intact). This roof had almost certainly been repaired and extended when the sheepfold was built. The hut in its original state would have been just high enough for a man to stand upright inside. It was laid out as a single room, 13 feet by 8, with a low south-facing doorway the main source of light.

About a mile to the north is another ruin: the remains of what was to have been a silo to house Blue Streak ballistic missiles, the United Kingdom's only attempt to develop its own independent land-based nuclear weapons programme. Plans to construct a silo were set in motion in the mid-1950s, but had not progressed very far when it was found that the site, deemed politically feasible owing to its remoteness, was geologically problematic. The bedrock was so close to the surface that it would have been prohibitively expensive and time-consuming to drill deep enough for the entire 150-ft launching tube to be concealed below ground, while there was serious doubt as to whether the tube's embedded concrete base could withstand the blast of take-off without melting. By 1958 the plan was to dig only a little way down, so that four-fifths of the tube would be visible above the surface – hidden at least in part by the valley sides, from which a ramp or causeway would probably have been extended to a point level with the silo tip. Loading rocket fuel also proved difficult. The liquid oxygen needed to be pumped in immediately before launching, as it could not be stored on board for long without icing up; this meant that the estimated time from alert to launch would have been four and a half minutes, unless a pair of missiles, one ready-fuelled and the other on standby, were to be deployed in turns every ten hours. The Macmillan government scrapped the project in 1960. Many people living locally were aware that a rocket-testing facility was being prepared, but assumed it had something to do with space exploration, and such was the government's anxiety to prevent any hint of the truth from leaking out that the construction area was completely cleared and close-planted with fir trees. The surviving ruins would now be almost as hard to trace as those of the worst-preserved shielings nearby; there is a length of sluice channel with concrete and steel linings, some heaps of excavated earth, and a water-filled hole 32 metres in diameter, with a few shuttering boards across its edges. Elsewhere nearby, and in much better repair, are several large firing test platforms, one of which was built right over the top of another group of ruined shielings, further thickening the palimpsest-landscape from which much of *The Oval Window* seems to take bearings. The whole area lies within the domain of RAF Spadeadam; it is now used for electronic weapons training, and is under strict Ministry of Defence control, as was politely pointed out to me when I attempted to explore it.

The poem has a thread of imagery strongly suggestive of nuclear devastation, a 'thermal patchwork' (see p. 92 of this volume) of recurrent fires, sun and stone boiling, faces burning, snow, frost, deep cold, 'darkness by day' (p. 140), apocalyptic visions and premonitions, with survivors perhaps combing through 'the spoil and waste in a white suit' (p. 122). Another thread points to various forms of surveillance, military or otherwise ('Police aware', 'watches at point of entry', 'looking on', 'stands down'), or to operational codes and shorthands: 'smart guidance' (p. 90) indicates a laser or satellite projectile lock-on system, 'brevet clients on call' (p. 112) seems to refer to rapidly necessitated battlefield promotions, while 'blue to blue over' (p. 104) hints at a radio signal, or even a distress warning about friendly fire. For transhumance and its associated practices, the trace in the poem is more occluded and harder to grasp. In part, though, it may be lodged in repetition itself, beating out a path. Most of the poem's linguistic events occur twice, sometimes more often, helping to build a wider sense of 'coming through with your back turned' (p. 94), an underlying rhythm or pattern of outward and reverse, cyclical and rotatory movement; the words 'back' and 'turn' themselves make significant contributions to this pattern, from 'leads back' in the first stanza, to 'waiting for the turn' in the last, with other recurrent vocabulary lending support: 'cycle', 'fold', 'end-up', 'up-ended' – together with a mention of 'invertible counterpoint', a musical technique where the upper voice takes on the role of the lower and vice versa. At certain points these threads themselves seem to cross and intertwine. At that mention of 'smart guidance', for example:

> smart guidance *ex* stock
> makes for home like a cup cake over

a suggestion of safe and skilful passage along the settled route of seasonal migration is just detectable, I think, within all the other things these words and phrases might signify, whether that be another field radio report, of a missile successfully locking on to its target, or a police intercom, or even some *Good Housekeeping*-style advice about basic hospitality requirements. Later on, in the lines

> each following suit
> by check according to rote
>   (p. 110)

an established and habituated cultural process seems to slip in and out of focus with an authoritarian control system.

At one level, in keeping with the topography of *The Oval Window*, such instances might simply represent the imposition of brutal armed force upon archaic sustaining sources. This would connect with the poem's passing mention of the story of Erysichthon, from Ovid's *Metamorphoses*:

> wounds were his feast,
> his life to life a prey.[1]
>   (p. 106)

Erysichthon, king of Thessaly, violated a grove sacred to the goddess Demeter; ignoring her protests and those of some of his own men, he hacked down the hallowed trees to build a feasting hall. For this, his punishment was to be afflicted with a hunger so insatiable that, after fruitlessly consuming everything he could find, he was driven to start eating himself, gnawing his own flesh in grim parody of the feast he had intended. In the same stanza of *The Oval Window* this passage is closely followed by a line from the Book of Numbers:

> Spring up, O well; sing unto it

---

1. *Metamorphoses*, VIII; translated by Thomas Vernon, in *Ovid's Metamorphoses, translated into English verse under the direction of Sir Samuel Garth, by Mr Dryden, Mr Addison, and other eminent hands* (London, 1717). Prynne made further reference to this myth in the poem 'Marzipan', in *Bands Around the Throat* (1987), whose closing lines read 'Ten thousand / families in the mountains, starved / on mountain grass: and made me eat / both gravel, dirt and mud, and last / of all, to gnaw my flesh and blood.' J.H. Prynne, *Poems* (Bloodaxe Books, 2015), p. 348.

In the course of their wanderings in the wilderness, Moses and the Israelites came to Beer, that is, 'well': 'the well wherof the Lord spake unto Moses, Gather the people together, and I will give them water. / Then Israel sang this song, Spring up, O well; sing ye unto it: / The princes digged the well, the nobles of the people digged it, by the direction of the lawgiver, with their staves.'[2] In one allusion, trees are felled and the land leached bare of nourishment; in the other, the conditions for the revival of life are found in a desert, miraculously uncovered by communal singing and labour: a striking juxtaposition, near the centre of the poem, of the ravaging and the creating of consecrated sites. This is then immediately followed by a series of mordant puns made possible by the way the jargon of the financial markets makes metaphorical use of physical nourishment and pre-industrial subsistence: 'pool', 'prime hock', 'pump', etc.

But where the primary focus is on so hastily-assembled and transient a building as a hut, the relationship between creating and ravaging is more ambiguous. In his 2008 essay on huts and poetry,[3] Prynne described how such places already encompass both pastoral-ceremonious and military-aggressive elements; huts have from ancient times been associated not just with shepherds and cattle-pastures, but with the presence of occupying troops, rapidly and temporarily deployed, whose very hut-dwelling would itself mark their alienation from the surrounding locale and its communities. (In this regard, the present-day military takeover of the old Tinkler Crags shieling ground might actually seem strangely appropriate.) Huts of this kind, instead of being end-stations on traditional and settled routes over a landscape, would effectively establish a provisional or demountable barrier across the landscape, a threshold point from which one cultural order might warily, contemptuously, or wistfully survey the domestic practices of another – in which connection the lines 'smart guidance ex stock / makes for home' seem to be sending more and more possibilities rippling out.

Either way, rural huts, by their very nature as outposts, are often likely to be found in marginal or frontier positions, militarised or not – the Tinkler Crags site is very close to the England-Scotland border – where any enforced separation inevitably carries an implicit potential for meeting and mingling.

---

2. Numbers 21: 16-18.

3. 'Huts', *Textual Practice* 22:4 (2008), 613-33.

Prynne's essay is really an extended meditation on this 'dual aspect' of huts, their capacity to represent both 'benign and hostile shelter, human life simple and serene or under ominous threat'.[4] Virtually every sentence in this essay seems to resonate in some manner with *The Oval Window*, from the identification of the hut in Collins's 'Ode to Evening' as a shieling, to the discussion of the meeting between Paul Celan and Heidegger at the latter's celebrated *Berghütte*, a purpose-built mountainside retreat in the Black Forest.[5] The line 'Last light foams / at this crest' (p. 130), coming at the point where *The Oval Window* actually makes mention of the Tinkler Crags shieling, would certainly seem to be remembering Collins:

> be mine the Hut,
> That from the Mountain's Side,
> Views Wilds, and swelling Floods,
> And Hamlets brown, and dim-discover'd Spires,
> And hears their simple Bell, and marks o'er all
> Thy Dewy Fingers draw
> The gradual dusky Veil.[6]

That is to say, Prynne's line remembers the 'Ode to Evening', while intimating a more sinister sense of imminent extinction, from which a poet would not be able to maintain so safe a distance. Meanwhile, in respect of 'human life simple and serene', Prynne's essay also discusses the idea that certain kinds of pastoral hut, precisely by their primal nature, their being built at the verges of viable existence, might allow for or promote particular forms of communitarianism, of the free exchange or equal sharing of labour and return. The essay's main reference in this regard is to the Siberian hut-dwelling tribes studied in the late nineteenth century by the anarchist Peter Kropotkin, who saw them as models for a non-competitive, co-operative society. But at the time *The Oval Window* was being written a different if comparable set of ethnographic researches was involved in the compositional underlay: Sandra

---

4. 'Huts', *Textual Practice*, 22.4 (2008), p. 624.

5. It is hard not to think that Celan must have been struck by this hut's structural resemblances to concentration camp housing.

6. William Collins, 'Ode to Evening' (1746), *ll.* 34-40; 'Huts', pp. 613-16.

Ott's *The Circle of Mountains* (1981), a study of a Souletine Basque community still at that time practising transhumance in the Pyrenees. This community seemed to have established an almost complete co-operative equality by organising their entire way of life upon a concept of rotation and turn-taking, mimicking at the level of the smallest daily social practices the cyclical, out-and-back movements of the transhumant migration:

> each following suit
> by check according to rote
> (p. 110)

Similar principles to those governing village life were reproduced among the shepherds living in huts at the summer pastures (in Basque, the *olha*). A specified set of tasks and duties, from general servant to master cheese-maker, was distributed among as many as six shepherds, who would take turns to perform each role, moving up a step at specified intervals to the next role, whereupon the one who had completed his cheese-making would leave the hut to be replaced by a fresh 'servant' newly-arrived from the village below, and so on. As Ott describes it, 'during the period of summer transhumance, the shepherds are said to be "in the *olha* rotation" [...] The shepherds are conceived as moving up and down and from left to right as they ascend and descend; they rotate in a clockwise direction'.[7] In *The Oval Window* one might catch a glimpse of transhumant shepherd life, with or without religious or elegiac overtones, in the line 'Not lost from the track as passing its peak' (p. 106); or even, distantly, in the phrase 'cycle time' (p. 100), which on industrial assembly lines refers to the period required for the worker to complete a process before the unit of work is passed on. 'Smoke from inside the hut' (p. 134) could be a sign of human presence, as in 'Tintern Abbey' (or, of course, the aftermath of destruction). The Tinkler Crags huts, like those in the Pyrenees, would have had open fires laid on the stone floor, and wood-smoke would have continuously pervaded the building – a small instance of the discomforts and hardships of such existence which, as the huts essay stresses, impose relentless pressure on the idea of the 'serene' and simple life

---

7. Sandra Ott, *The Circle of Mountains* (Oxford: Oxford University Press, 1981), p. 156.

in an alternative social and economic order. The realities of poverty and deprivation break more directly into the poem also. The phrase 'three to one herring' (p. 122), for example, in a kind of ironic allusion to Biblical parable, was a common rural formula, well-known in East Anglia, to signify a family so poor they had to manage on a single fish shared between them. Similarly, 'its porridge bowl' (p. 106) suggests scant nourishment serving several people, this time perhaps with a more specifically Scottish slant (see below). An air of hopelessness and compulsion drifts through much of the imagery and phrasing ('at a loss', 'falling short', 'fluffed and spilled', 'bond market', 'enslaved non-stop', etc.), while most striking in respect of this particular thread are the poem's two references to Eric Richards's study of the Highland Clearances, one reference including the hypnotising detail of a cottager's helping to demolish a neighbour's dwelling:

> when the furniture was removed
> he pulled out the window-frames, pulled down
> the roof, and pushed in the walls
>   (p. 108)

The verbatim transfer of these lines into the poem gives them such a momentum of angry, desperate protest that it is disconcerting to find their original context to be one of apparently calm acceptance: two options, 'each' perhaps 'framing the other' (p. 136), arising at a moment 'when hope is gone' (p. 130).

Elsewhere, *The Oval Window* seems to touch on another element in Prynne's longstanding interest in pastoral and transhumant cultures, the belief that lyric poetry itself developed from earlier traditions of communal singing. Such singing would be performed at least in part to offer relief from the strains and exertions of collective labour, in work songs or marching songs, and in part to help organise that labour *as* collective, by setting strict rhythms for it. Aspects of these ideas seem to coalesce in the lines

> From each
> throat at its fan opening they spoke out
> their force of numbers
>   (p. 104)

where the word 'numbers' just carries the sense of strophic choral chanting, a sense peeping out from among all the other things these lines could mean –

including, again, a military counterpart to the communal voice, a parade ground call-and-response or numbering-off.[8] This oral tradition is a central concern of Prynne's 2007 commentary on Wordsworth's poem 'The Solitary Reaper',[9] another recent critical essay involving many tacit backward glances at *The Oval Window*. In his commentary Prynne explores, with extraordinary tenacity, the range of significance released by Wordsworth's imaginary encounter with a Highland girl, who, singing while she 'cuts, and binds the grain', becomes a representative of poetry's ancient provenance: '[T]o the startled poet she must surely be a primal muse-figure, as Ceres herself, because her song is the basis of lyric and its original roots in the life and work of a human community' (*Field Notes*, p. 25). For Prynne, such an encounter as Wordsworth records would pose a profound, implicitly admonitory challenge to the imagination of the modern, isolated, print-culture poet. It is essentially an encounter with a world felt to be deeply connected to one's own, but from which one is now alienated in every conceivable way: by education, by language-barrier, by 'modernity' widely considered, or by class affiliation; in this instance the dominant political and national interest to which the poet cannot help but belong would be actively contributing to the terminal decline of the way of life from which the reaper's singing derives. In the face of all this, Wordsworth 'can neither give up being a poet nor cross the divide into her threatened world [...] so that her solitude echoes by deep resonance with his own' (*Field Notes*, p. 10); the challenge is to do some justice to the power of the experience and its contradictions without diluting or appropriating them.

'Echoes' and 'resonance' establish a vocabulary here, since although the initial gesture in 'The Solitary Reaper' is to the visual field ('Behold her'), the full force of the experience is auditory:

> O listen! for the vale profound
> Is overflowing with the sound.

---

8. At the time the poem was written, Prynne had been interested in the work of Jacqueline Duchemin, herself a Basque, whose 1960 study *La Houlette et la Lyre* put forward perhaps the most elaborate claim that music, song and poetry originated in and was tightly bound to the shepherd life of the ancient world – a claim that found however few supporters among other classical scholars.

9. *Field Notes: The Solitary Reaper and Others* (Cambridge 2007).

It is within this sonic inundation that meaning is really felt to gather. Prynne devotes a good deal of discussion in *Field Notes* to the kind of intent and active listening which would allow the reaper's 'presence and its musical overflow to [...] enter consciousness at an altogether deeper, more fundamental level of understanding' (*Field Notes*, p. 72). The consequence of such listening 'could almost be like being re-born, into this world and its real truth' (p. 15). There are two specific references to Wordsworth in *The Oval Window*, both of which, without addressing the issue of active listening directly, engage with conditions that would implicitly support it – a cutting-out of ambient distraction, an initial or background stillness, with the additional requirement that the 'inner life of subject-feeling' be 'quietened and placed in suspense' (*Field Notes*, p. 88). Hence, 'Calm is all nature as a resting wheel' (p. 138), from the 'Sonnet: Written in Very Early Youth', and the 'silent fire' (p. 112) which 'virtue feeds', in *The Excursion* – 'A calm, a beautiful, and silent fire / From the encumbrances of mortal life'. But of course the whole of Prynne's poem must at some level be predicated upon the actual physiology of listening, since it is the 'oval window' itself, the threshold point between the middle and the inner ear, through which sound waves pass to be converted into electrical impulses in the brain, that makes any such Wordsworthian revelation possible. And by the time *The Oval Window* reaches its climax, it is as if all the disparate auditory events that have floated through it – cries, hums, singing, speech, murmurs, echoes – have gathered into a single burst of sound:

> Standing by the window I heard it,
> while waiting for the turn
>   (p. 142)

'It' carries an unmistakable epiphanic force. Perhaps, rather than Wordsworth, the first line might recall Arnold's 'Dover Beach', with its suggestion of a stoic facing of bleak realities; but either way it is the ear, hearing and listening to things, that would seem to have brought us at last to an apprehension of some fundamental condition of being, 'the crossing flow / of even life', found here at the farthest reach of travel, at an edge or threshold point where one domain opens on another, in a pause before 'the turn'. This 'crossing flow' would presumably never cease, although we may only rarely and through intense ritualistic preparation be able to hear it; and the 'turn' when it came could be truly apocalyptic, an unprecedented transformation of experience and the world, or, alternatively, the resumption of something already anticipated – like the imminent turn of that 'resting wheel', which even as it rests intimates the rotatory movement on which it will sooner or later re-embark. It is a moot point whether Prynne may have been remembering that phrase 'the crossing flow / of even life', when more than twenty years later he wrote à propos 'The Solitary Reaper' of an 'unobstructed confluence of recognition' (*Field Notes*, p. 89); or whether the further idea in *Field Notes* that all sense of 'before and after' would be suspended, 'held in abeyance' in active listening (p. 88) might look back to *The Oval Window*'s enigmatic epigraphs, where programming language seems to lift the very words BEFORE and AFTER away from their normal function as temporal markers. These preoccupations certainly appear deep and prolonged enough to allow for some occluded self-quoting. As for Wordsworth's being 're-born' from his experience (*Field Notes*, p.15), *The Oval Window* has 'newly born', at a natural divide in the poem, just past the middle:

> We go over. The dip stands down
>   in the oval window, in
> the blackened gutter stop of the newly born.
>   (p. 122)

A gutter stop diverts a flow into a fresh channel, while 'blackened' might carry a suggestion of the previous flow's accumulated, congealed deposits. These particularly mysterious and haunting lines reawaken the military language ('stands down') while giving it a strange visionary stillness, and at the same time offering a more literal sense, a glimpse of landscape contours sloping away into a valley, just as one might in fact see them through the opening in the wall at Tinkler Crags [fig. 9].

Anatomical description of the ear makes it sound like a rudimentary building: it has two windows, oval and round, a floor, a foot-piece, a roof, a ridge, a vestibule, an anterior wall and a posterior wall. In Prynne's photographs of the shieling site, it is almost as if the stone equivalents of these features have been picked out one by one for inspection. The shots are various: some of the full horizon; some sharp close-ups, from numerous minutely-adjusted angles, of intricate dry-stone patterns; some which set the remains more proportionately in the terrain their builders chose for them – doorways opening to the south for maximum light, the long axes of the ground plans lying east-west, the shelter of the steep eastern valley side, the gentle slope down to the stream.

One or two of these latter pictures might prompt the reader's imagination to reconstruct and repopulate the scene. But the long views and extreme close-ups seem more powerfully estranging, as do the snapshots of the detritus of more modern pasturage, rusting gates, barbed wire and corrugated roofing, strewn among the ruins as evidence of the new uses to which they have been put, uses in many cases themselves already superseded: a reminder that these photographs were taken well over thirty years ago and constitute a historic record of a site doubtless still steadily crumbling away.

But perhaps in addition one could hazard that the sheer scope and intensity of this photographic record (of which the sample included in this volume is only a fraction) might be speaking of a kind of compulsion on Prynne's part not unlike that which the huts essay attributed to Wordsworth[10] and Collins: literally, to go to the hut, deliberately to seek out the place where the partition between shelter and exposure is at its thinnest and most attenuated, and to enact there a late-20th century version of that Romantic encounter with the unaccommodated wild, or the wellsprings of imagination, however variously construed — the encounter which, as the 'Huts' essay concludes by saying, remains at some level an essential prerequisite for poetry at all times. In this case, moreover, the hut is so ruined, virtually down to the bare single wall with the oval-shaped opening in it (as seen in fig. 9), that any clear distinction between shelter and exposure, between inside and outside, seems to have collapsed almost completely; it would be hard to tell simply from 'standing by the window' whether one was inside looking out or outside looking in. It all constitutes, so to speak, an image of maximum permeability within the spectrum of processes in which matter is continually re-formed: as with the sky seen from 'either side' of this window, everything here 'runs in and out and over' (p. 130), in unrestricted backwards and forwards motion.[11] In the final stanza, the lines

---

10. Not specifically 'The Solitary Reaper' on this occasion, but a fragment of blank verse provisionally titled 'Incipient Madness'; 'Huts', 622-4.

11. This play of 'either side', or 'on both sides', is oddly complemented by the photograph on the poem's original front cover in 1983, which was (probably inadvertently) printed from a mirror-image of the negative, appearing to show a view of the window from the north, but actually taken from the south and reversed. The only true shot from the north side clearly shows modern corrugated roof-sheeting attached to the wall just below the window opening, as in fig. 16.

Free

to leave at either side, at the fold line

pick up again the idea of unchecked movement across a boundary, or the crest of a gradient ('passing its peak'), from where, once 'we go over', our track might alter course; the 'fold line' could signify any of the more or less porous borders and barriers with which the poem is supplied (including the outline of the actual sheepfold attached to the remains of the hut wall, as in fig. 17). We might also have a sense of a fold line in the typographical layout of page 118, where fragments of phrases seem to be reaching towards and falling away from a central ridge or gully, phrases forming and dissolving on either side, at times seemingly prompted by but insecurely attached to each other. This section itself could equally constitute the poem's own fold line, situated at a central dividing mark between 'the turn for good' (p. 116) and the more expansive writing that follows it, in which images of birth, beginnings, and exposure to the elements mingle with a building lexicon (eave, rim, purlin, tenon), joining, parting, and 'the bud of ruin', a compound of growth and decay. One phrase among those fragments does seem however to turn back across the page's gully, into a kind of coherence:

so on, go on

to the lammas

As mentioned above, Lammas Day, August 1st, traditionally marked the end of the summer transhumance in the north of England and elsewhere, when the pastoral community would abandon the huts and begin to retrace their steps back towards the winter settlement: hence they would only 'go on' as far as the farthest edge or turning point of the cycle. At the same time, there might seem to be something unremitting here in the repetitions of 'on', an implacable pressure which could put one in mind of the term 'latter-lammas', with its apocalyptic connotations of the last day: end of season and end of world, distantly entwining again the poem's pastoral thread with its nuclear-destructive counterpart.

The tentative pursuit of any such threads leaves of course the bulk of the poem more or less untouched. Reading perspectives continually shift, and none could be remotely comprehensive. The implicitly Wordsworthian direction of this discussion could readily be challenged, for example, by the massed quotations from Chinese lyrics which dominate the second half of *The*

Oval Window; lyrics which, as Richard Kerridge mentions in his essay, often sound in English translation as if Wordsworth could have written them, but which actually belong to a compositional tradition running almost directly counter to Western Romanticism.

But if *The Oval Window* does have a Wordsworthian stimulus, perhaps it derives from a passage in Dorothy Wordsworth's *Recollections of a Tour made in Scotland*, just prior to her inclusion in her text of the first version of 'The Solitary Reaper'. Walking the hill track leading from Loch Ketterine (now Katrine) towards Loch Voil, she and William came to

> several deserted mountain huts or shiels, and rested for some time beside one of them, upon a hillock of its green plot of monumental herbage. Wm. here threw off a stanza for the beginning of an ode upon the affecting subject of those relics of human society found in that grand and solitary region.[12]

This particular 'ode' appears never to have been written. But would it be too fanciful to see *The Oval Window* as at least in part a realisation, 180 years on, of what Wordsworth had left unfinished?

N.H. REEVE

---

12. Dorothy Wordsworth, *Recollections of a Tour made in Scotland (A.D. 1803)*, in *Journals of Dorothy Wordsworth*, ed. E. De Selincourt, vol. 1, London: Macmillan & Co, 1952, p. 379. The 'green plot', as in other such references, would mark the spot where the livestock had been milked near the door.

www.ingramcontent.com/pod-product-compliance
Lightning Source LLC
Jackson TN
JSHW052136131224
75386JS00039B/1286